THE BEST OF INDIAN SPORTS WRITING

Editor Sundeep Misra

wisdom tree

Cover Photograph: Taken at SCG, 3rd Day, Australia vs India, 4 January 2008. Available under Creative Commons GNU Free Documentation License. © 2008, Privatemusings.

First published 2013

ISBN 978-81-8328-292-5

Published by

Wisdom Tree
4779/23, Ansari Road
Darya Ganj, New Delhi-110 002
Ph.: 23247966/67/68
wisdomtreebooks@gmail.com

Printed in India

To Satwant and Durga
Prassana Misra

Contents

Introduction

Sundeep Misra

It was my first scrapbook. I was just ten years old and on the cover I had pasted, painstakingly cut from *The Statesman*, pictures of Sriram Singh and Alberto Juantorena at the 1976 Montreal Olympics. Inside the book was a picture I still hold dear, like it's been xeroxed into my brain—a young Edwin Moses hurdling on the turn, the bobbing gold necklace reaching up to his chin, his dark glasses making him out to be this superhero phantom gliding over the hurdles. Inside the pages was also a bearded, emancipated figure of Finland's long distance hero Lasse Viren. That was the first time I read about blood doping and how Viren may have stepped on the other side of the law to acquire two gleaming gold medals in the 5,000 m and 10,000 m races. Those were the days of *The Sportsweek*, *The Statesman* and *The Illustrated Weekly* that brought out specials on events like the Olympics and the football World Cup. Any written word was swallowed and stored away. Pele came to now Kolkata with the Cosmos team and *The Statesman* brought out a six-page special. It still remains in a steel trunk at home.

There was no television those days. You just read. Read till you had the entire sports page by rote. Fast forward to the 1982 football World Cup in Spain. BBC Sports Special announced Brazil had been ambushed 3-2 by Italy. The dream was over. There would be no Socrates, Zico, Junior or Falcao in the World Cup final. Yet I thought maybe, just maybe, the BBC guys had made a mistake. The newspapers would probably correct it the following morning. No. The headline on the front page screamed 'Brazil shocked; football fans mourn'. I read and re-read the defensive lapses and how many times Socrates and Falcao came close to scoring. BBC gave a highlights package at night and all I could hear was—'It's Socrates, Zico, Falcao in front; oh, what a miss; its Eder now with Socrates; Zico has it.' Thrice they announced Paolo Rossi's name and he scored a hat-trick.

Once in college, *The Times, London*, *The Observer* and *The Independent* became a staple diet for their amazing sports coverage. Sydney Friskin, writing on hockey for *The Times*, gave you an insight into writing that perfect match report even if both teams had drawn 6-6 and you had twelve goals to describe. Friskin had that ability to keep the copy clean and transport you into the heart of the match; you could hear the crowd, the thwack of stick on ball, the referee's whistle and the cheers of the players. Sitting with him over a glass of beer in Berlin during the 1995 Champions Trophy, I asked him to share the secret of his writing. He said, 'Writing is not just putting words on paper. Sport is simple, keep the writing simple. Describe it like a kid would after watching a match. Remember the reader hasn't seen the match—the sports page is the stadium and your words the match.'

Friskin died on 26 November 1999, at the age of eighty-four, a year before the Sydney Olympic Games. During his last few years, sports writing was already evolving. Now readers were watching live matches and then reading sports pages or sports magazines. A whole new bunch of writers now jostled for space with the established ones.

The long form of journalism, so popular throughout the world, is dying in India. Everything is slowly becoming statistics-based; sports writing is following the T20 path. Gone are the essays, sports stories are like takeaways. One quote is enough to inspire a 300-word 'article', also labelled an 'exclusive'. No more research, just Google-search and a phone call are enough to drum up a story. Sadly, sports editors have obliged; the pages are finished early. One evening after finishing a 1200 word story on how a champion school hockey team was refused a grant by a sports body, I sent the story to the desk. The next morning, I was horrified to see the story was not even 400 words. The bottom had not been cut, it was hacked off. The explanation: 'You need to write a story where the introduction says it all.' I did argue, 'But this was a one-off story. I interviewed ten people and could have probably written close to 2000 words. I fought for that space.'

The answer—'Readers don't have so much time.' That was back in 1994. Not much has changed. It's probably got worse.

In a conversation with Wisdom Tree's publisher Shobit Arya, I spoke about the lack of a sports magazine that simply tells its writers, just go ahead and write, don't bother about the words. He said, 'Why not an anthology?'

The selection of writers was tough. Most of the writers in the anthology are the kind who would like to bowl a forty-five over spell. Not for them, the four-over, bend your shoulder and waltz home.

For those who read *The Hindu*, S Thyagarajan is a legend. If you get him talking—and I can assure you it would be easier for the Indian hockey team to win gold at the Olympics than expect Thyagarajan to open his Pandora's box of hockey stories and those countless Olympic and World Cup games he has covered—just don't get him to discuss that tragic November day of 1982, his story in this anthology. It is a day even Thyagarajan wouldn't want to remember.

Then there were those who had left sports writing, even though they were good at it. Mudar Patherya, a former *Sportsworld* journalist and now an investment adviser, has written on his place of homage: the Eden Gardens at Kolkata. Rohit Brijnath flew off to Australia after a longish stint in this country but thankfully came back to Singapore to renew his writing on sport. He sent in his offering, 'Man of Bronze'. In the 'Last of the Romantics', Suresh Menon, one of India's finest cricket writers, says, 'Dravid might have to wait before his true worth is realised.' Some of the other entries are by KP Mohan, ever the fact seeking man, on PT Usha; Arindam Basu on the barefoot footballers and Partha Bhaduri on 'The Bastard Child'. Sriram Dayanand, a cricket writer from Toronto, Canada, writes on the Chinnaswamy Stadium; Shantanu Guha Ray on a village in Jharkhand called Rukka; Ayaz Memon on how the cricket world was turned upside down; Sukhwant Basra, who drilled forehands as a kid, now follows the story of Leander Paes in 'Me, Doc and the BATboy'. Kamesh Srinivasan has written on 'Perfection is Not a Chimera'; Sandeep Nakai on the Perfect Epitaph; Anand Philar on his love for the F1 circuit at Sepang, Sharda Ugra on cricket in Kashmir and Clayton Murzello on his emotional meeting with a wheelchair-bound West Indian pace bowler Winston Davis.

A huge amount of credit to Nandini Gupta at Wisdom Tree for keeping the anthology alive and to the invisible hand, Nandita Bhardwaj, for going through the text. To Shobit Arya, for believing that tomorrow was the new deadline. To all the writers who agreed to contribute and ensure that India's first anthology on sports writing went to print, my gratitude.

And to Sydney Friskin, a big thank you for allowing me to spend those hours understanding sport, as you clattered away on a typewriter.

Bastard Child Takes Centre Stage

Partha Bhaduri

> The crescendo rose as India played South Africa for a spot in the semi-finals. The hosts were unbeaten, being touted as red-hot favourites, the unheralded, self-proclaimed progenitors of the format reclaiming their own. Shaun Pollock joked, perhaps untimely, 'I don't think there's time to choke.'

Sometimes, moments stick out like sore thumbs.

At other times they pass us by, casually and cruelly, till we realise it's too late for a backward glance. For a sports journalist, such moments are everyday occurrence. Often, sport is a fleeting metaphor for life: throbbing in the present, swaying to the surety of clear-cut goals, victory or defeat; yet pulsating, at all times, with shades of grey.

A sports chronicler must live in those moments, feeling for the pulse of a contest till work and play blur into each other. Mostly, the skill and physicality, or the dopamine rush of a tactical masterstroke, linger on like the ghost of electricity, like some vague aftertaste prised from the haze of memory. Often, it's coloured by opinion or number-crunching fixations, or maybe rare statistical insight.

And then, of course, there are those moments which become monsters, bigger than the sum of their parts, shaped by human hands or sporting magic or the tide of the times. Often all three.

This is one of those moments.

I don't want to play spoilsport but such esoteric thoughts were far from my mind when I landed in Johannesburg in September 2007 for the inaugural, and oddly titled, ICC World T20, a World Cup of cricket which wasn't a cricket World Cup. It seemed a bastard child of the new age, seeking to walk a few steps without tottering. A phoenix rising from the ashes of a disastrous fifty-over World Cup in the Caribbean, held earlier that year.

It turned out to be a tournament chock full of fresh 'aha' moments which no one had anticipated. At that time, no one quite knew what to make of it all and the whole lead-up was one big red ball of irony. In the context of what eventually transpired, it's all too quickly forgotten how vehemently opposed India's cricket board was to the idea of a twelve-team World T20.

Perhaps they were swayed by the small but extremely influential coterie of senior Indian batsmen who thought there was no future in the format. That it was a mere fly-by-night whim, a perfect tonic for stale English audiences which had lapped up the three-hour game redesigned as family entertainment, but wholly unworkable in the Indian arena.

Their outlook mirrored that of the cricket intelligentsia, which has always scoffed at new-fangled means of roping in audiences and has caustically disapproved of makeovers. These naysayers haven't had much impact on the history of the game, considering cricket's constant tweakings right from the days of timeless Tests to a five-day cap on proceedings. Maybe, modern Test cricket as we know it was the first T20, figuratively speaking.

Some of these reservations would be proved true as T20 took root with the Indian Premier League (IPL), but it had nothing to do with spectator fatigue and we're jumping ahead of ourselves. As it turned out, these leading Indian batsmen opted out, perhaps to make way for the new generation in a format tailor-made for short attention spans. The Board of Control for Cricket in India (BCCI) was outvoted 10-1 by the other full International Cricket Council (ICC) members and confirmed participation. To everyone's surprise, MS Dhoni was named captain and he took to the job like he was born for it.

T20 traced its roots back to England and Wales, where the first such game at Lord's—between Middlesex and Surrey in 2004—attracted the largest audience for any county game in three decades. On the English county circuit, the three-hour game of cricket suddenly rejuvenated stale audiences (it was a mere momentary blip), helping redesign an arguably snooty game as family entertainment.

Venues in India could not have beer vendors, bouncy castles, speed guns or trick-or-treaters, argued the BCCI. Forget about picnic hampers or cameras, at the Eden Gardens security guards will even slice an apple before you can take it inside. There were other, cricketing, concerns: Pundits screamed blue murder at a batsman's game tilting even more towards the way of the batsmen.

Everyone was jumping ahead of themselves. In truth, the T20 wave had not even begun. Even though the rebel Indian Cricket League (ICL) had announced its presence, T20 wasn't mainstream yet, at least not in the manner it was to become. The wave began with India's twin wins over Pakistan in that tournament, reaching a crescendo with that final in Johannesburg. Midway through a young

India's dream run, though, the T20 monster had already ballooned out of proportion, threatening to chew up all in its path, pushing fans out on the streets in droves from Durban to Delhi and consuming media and public imagination like nobody's business.

As even the United States woke up to it, the inaugural World T20 went from being a merely successful tournament to a spectacular one, with far-reaching commercial ramifications for the sport.

The scales tilted at Kingsmead, when Yuvraj Singh hit his six sixes against England, a knock which did more for T20 and its mega-riches than all the other knocks combined. The final against Pakistan was the icing on the cake. A certain Mr Lalit Modi watched every game like a hawk, often quietly sitting in the media box and asking journalists what they made of it all.

I was there soaking it all in, frenetically writing my daily reports through a crazed fortnight of blurry eyes, constant travel, insane deadlines and enormous fun.

It all began at Mumbai airport, where Virender Sehwag stood alone with his luggage, a forlorn figure looking to reboot his flagging career, a precursor of the calm before the storm. He would join the rest of the jet-lagged squad (flying in from England) in Johannesburg. Everyone thought the format was tailor-made for him but Sehwag wasn't so sure.

India had played only one T20 International before the tournament, itineraries were jampacked and a new captain and stand-in manager/coach in Lalchand Rajput had no time to strategise. The Indian team, literally, had no time to unpack.

Apart from an occasional hoarding, Johannesburg was strangely quiet when I landed three days before the start. The tournament had already got off to a controversial start with Shoaib Akhtar being sent home for hitting teammate Mohammad Asif with a bat. It was only a day before the event that the city seemed to warm up.

The cheapest tickets were priced at a mere Rand 20 for games like Sri Lanka versus Kenya, while the opening game tickets were going for R60 to R120. It all seemed reasonable and ticket booths were closed a day before the start. They had sold out. The buzz was yet to build up.

I remember a group of eager fans posing with South Africa skipper Graeme Smith at the 'Bullring', then suddenly turning on some Indian reporters at the scene: 'Why couldn't Sachin Tendulkar have come?' South Africans, I also learnt, believed they were the proud pioneers for the format, not England. Tendulkar's absence was perceived as a personal insult, but soon they would find new Indian heroes in Yuvraj and Dhoni.

Meanwhile the cricketers, mostly non-Indians, were busy sending out feelers to the rebel ICL (Indian Cricket League) which Brian Lara had joined. Adam Gilchrist said at a press conference that he backed the idea, saying it would end ICC's monopoly on the game. Very soon, the ICL would become a pariah, with T20 becoming a darling of the establishment.

Everyone was still feeling for the change in the air and all the excitement was a welcome break from the staid monotony the one-day game had lapsed into. The opening day of the tournament, in retrospect, was where the IPL really began: An evening start, fireworks, serpentine queues at beer stalls, crazy fancy dresses and a quaint, village-fair ambience.

It all ensured the tournament got off to a rollicking start even before the players took the field. Bollywood-variety celebs mingled with commoners, the dancing girls started hating fours and sixes because it meant time to go to work and DJs pumped it up so loud one couldn't hear oneself think.

The South Africans soaked in the carnival atmosphere and fireworks, getting drunk and letting loose.

The opening night was one of those moments which made 11 September look good for the first time since 2001. Chris Gayle rose to the occasion, hitting a 57-ball 117 in the opening game—the first T20 century—and promptly saw his team lose to South Africa. T20 could be fun, and unpredictable. A 54-ball 90, like the one from Herschelle Gibbs' bat, proved more effective than Gayle's ton. Sure, it was a batsman's game and bowlers, it was clear, needed to be astute to prevent being mere lambs to the slaughter.

T20 may have proved to be a box-office hit but the players were still feeling their way. Very soon they were to figure out that slow and steady may not win you this game, but cold and clinical still might. Batting could win you a game, but bowling and fielding could lose it for you. MS Dhoni watched the first game and said, 'T20 is very demanding. You need too many plans in place.' Or none, for that matter.

It was such a nascent beast that records were being broken with every game. Gayle had made more than 57 per cent of the runs in his team's total. A combined total of thirteen bowlers were used by both sides. The opening match was marked by 36 fours, 18 sixes and 413 runs.

It numbed the senses, but the audience liked the high. The infant started crawling. The Indian cricket team was watching, learning on the go. So was the pack of Indian journalists, who were discovering T20 had its own challenges. The time difference with India meant copies had to land within seconds of the match getting over and the writing had to be real time, with the eyes watching, the fingers typing and the brain racing ahead of both! Over the course of the next two weeks, a bunch of young reporters would come of age, much like the format itself.

South Africa afforded its own charms, though, and the first half of the game could be spent watching from the stands, feeling the vibe, chatting up with passionate fans or making new friends, a luxury denied to journalists on Indian grounds. Personally, I had already survived a moment of panic, having lost my accreditation card, the special pass for journalists, after the first game. Amid the endless packing and unpacking it disappeared, the worst sin! I was sure I had kept it somewhere safe, but three of my roommates turned everything upside down and it still couldn't be found. Luckily, a rush to the ICC office and some friendly banter helped tide over the crisis, a duplicate being issued in no time.

The Indian cricketers, meanwhile, got going with their training sessions, the first of a precious few before their matches started and they stopped having nets altogether. At Centurion, Yuvraj Singh whacked a few balls out of the arena and solemnly declared, staring at his willow, '*Yeh* T20 bats *ke liye achcha nahi hai* (T20 isn't good for bats).' Sehwag said variations for bowlers would be the key, but Irfan Pathan, who had a very good tournament, felt otherwise. Dhoni was worried India's fielding might not be good enough, or flashy enough, to prevent opposition batsmen from taking off.

India's first game, a loosener against Scotland, was a bootie-shaking damp squib, being completely washed out. The inimitable Quinton Ribbonar, the leader of the cheerleaders, so to speak, was furious. 'We are as important as the weather when it comes to T20. We've brought the sex back into the game,' he declared, puffing away to glory before dancing in the rain. A few hours later, the cricketers would have a new distraction: Rahul Dravid decided to step down as skipper back home, making for reams of speculative newsprint, even as the game against Pakistan loomed. One Pakistani player said, 'If they have any sense they'll make Dhoni full-time skipper.'

Then came the day of the diaspora. And a cricket match which India won 3-0! On the day of the India-Pakistan game, Durban resembled Delhi. That's an understatement; it was more Delhi than Delhi, an away outing which was like a home game for both teams.

One side of the stands was taken up by Pakistanis in green and on the other sat Indian fans in blue. Kingsmead resembled the Colloseum. The noise was deafening, the cheerleaders and DJs an unnecessary distraction. The contest had just got serious. By the end of the game, there were many who would have reminded themselves their heart was still beating.

The match, which ended in a tie, resulting in an absurd 'bowlout' victory for India, won the maximum-impact stakes. Irfan Pathan impressed. T20 made a grand entry and with one run needed from two balls, Pakistan's Misbah-ul-Haq messed up for the first time in the tournament, though memorably not the last. He couldn't connect off the first ball, barely connected off the second and that led to the bizarre sight of bowlers targeting empty stumps, a rule which would soon be rewritten. The unnecessary 'bowlout' gimmick apart, the game set the T20 ball rolling. Back home, Indians warmed up to an event which hadn't caught public fancy before this game.

Pakistan skipper Shoaib Malik declared with a straight face later he had no idea what the rule was all about, but his ignorance was overshadowed by the frenetic outpouring of joy from Indian fans. Durban poured out on the streets and MS Dhoni's post-match press conference was marred by shouts of 'Inquilaab zindabad'. For a while, a usually scary city became even more so. That was the first time organisers, spectators and players realised it was possible they were on to something with this T20 thing.

After a stopover at Johannesburg for a game against New Zealand which India lost, it was back to Durban. New Kiwi skipper Daniel Vettori proudly proclaimed that far from heralding the death of the spinner, the format would encourage slower bowlers. The tournament careened on, hurtling at breakneck speed. Brett Lee took a hat-trick. Kenya lost a game by 172 runs. Paul Collingwood apologised for lap-dancing his nights away and arriving back at his hotel on the morning of the game against South Africa. The Indians avoided such South African delights, grabbing whatever rest they could and mostly opting not to turn up for scheduled practice sessions, which miffed the ICC no end.

A vital game against England loomed. The Yuvraj Singh match. India had to win to stay alive and make the semis. On the day of the game, I went to the players' hotel to meet Harbhajan Singh and found Yuvraj in his room, heartily tucking into some roti and chicken. He was in a jovial, chatty mood, a man completely at ease with himself, completely oblivious to the fact that he was on the verge of a career-defining moment.

Meanwhile, Dhoni had learnt his captaincy was extended to the fifty-over game, but simply refused to talk. ICC officials told harassed Indian reporters, desperate for a byte, that they would get hold of a long-haired guy, shadow the face and make him parrot the expected lines! Thankfully Dhoni finally agreed to speak, so such out-of-the-box measures weren't put to the test! Harbhajan backed Dhoni's appointment, saying he was a thinking cricketer and all the seniors in the squad would back him.

That Pakistani cricketer back in Durban had known what he was talking about, after all.

In a couple of hours, everything—including Sehwag and Gambhir's early pyrotechnics—would be swamped by Yuvraj's savage, sublime effort that evening. It was exactly two weeks to the day Dmitri Mascarenhas had hit Yuvi's innocuous left-arm spin for five sixes and Freddie Flintoff didn't help matters by riling the batsman up on the field. A hapless Stuart Broad, the only seam bowler to have been hit for six sixes in the history of the game, unfortunately found himself in the way: the bowler's better judgement deserted him and Yuvraj was simply too good to be stopped. A photograph, the next morning, in a local daily showed a section of the crowd staring up in the sky at the ball, instead of down on the field.

Just before Yuvraj began the assault in the nineteenth over, Flintoff brushed past him. There seemed to be an ugly exchange, umpire Billy Doctrove intervened and the stage was set. The first six, longest of the lot, was smashed over wide long on. The second seemed to be a casual flick but it sailed over backward square. The third went over long off. By the time the fourth was hit, firecrackers were popping, Indian flags waving in the strong seafront breeze.

England had to pause. There was a team meeting, and a TV grab showed Stuart Broad, face pale, eyes popping out of his sockets, waiting for ideas. The fifth was a mishit over midwicket. Broad ran in with an air of inevitability. The sixth sailed over long on. No one, not the crowd, not the English team, not the millions hysterically screaming into their TV sets back home in India, could believe what had just happened. Yuvraj had scored his half-century off twelve balls.

Everyone who was there at the Kingsmead that day will tell you it was surreal. It was one of those ephemeral moments of sporting magic everyone is forever left groping for, including the star himself. As it turned out, without those six sixes, maybe India wouldn't have survived in the tournament and T20 wouldn't have taken wing the way it did. It is to the victimised Broad's credit that his career survived the evening's ferocity.

By this time, daily news of the World T20 made it regularly to the front pages of newspapers from India to South Africa to Pakistan to England. Talk of a brave, new India started doing the rounds and much of the credit went to MS Dhoni's astute captaincy, his rotation of bowlers and his ability to maximise the team's strengths. The crescendo rose as India played South Africa for a spot in the semi-finals. The hosts were unbeaten, touted as red-hot favourites, the unheralded, self-proclaimed progenitors of the format reclaiming their own. Shaun Pollock joked, perhaps untimely, 'I don't think there's time to choke.'

The words would bite him back, for providence was with India: Needing a mere 126 to qualify for the semis chasing 153, Graeme Smith's men ended up with 116. They choked in a major tournament, again. India found another future batting talent in Rohit Sharma, whose unbeaten half-century off forty balls proved invaluable. Dhoni himself chipped in with a 33-ball 45, and seamers RP Singh and Sreesanth did the rest. Smith promptly declared India would win the tournament. It was a statement made more to deflect his side's shortcomings than any real crystal-gazing insight.

By the next day, Sharma was the talk of the town, the new kid on the block everyone wanted more of. There were interviews to do in Marathi, English and Hindi, autographs to sign, a million hands to shake. He painstakingly explained to everyone he still had a way to go. Immersed in the moment, no one seemed to care.

With their entry into the semis it seemed India, as a sports team and as a nation, had temporarily taken over Durban. In a city where you normally can't walk down a few steps without the fear of being mugged, the safety of the tricolour was everywhere. Only Indian tourists can think of camping out in the open in a city like Durban and come away unscathed! One day, a fan who had flown in from Delhi—'for the final', he said—had the temerity to explain to Kevin Pietersen how the beautiful stretch of beach in front of the player's hotel was quite unsafe even for a jog in the mornings! The Pietermaritzburg-born KP, as everyone knows, is a Durban local and not given to too much patience. But he was so dumbstruck by the advice he took it all in, turned around and incredulously asked an Indian journalist, 'Is India very safe? I'm surprised.' Yes it is, better than here, he was told.

The Indian players, meanwhile, surprised even themselves with their performance. Confidence levels skyrocketed. It became clear, experience didn't matter much in T20 if you had a smart set of players and a thinking captain on board. Wonder of wonders, India's fielding, if not electric, was quietly spectacular: they had dropped a few but found the direct hits with eerie regularity. But could they do the unthinkable? Could they dethrone mighty Australia in the semis, ending a long-standing hegemony in ICC events? This wasn't 2003 anymore and the prospect didn't seem that unthinkable. After all, just a few days earlier a twenty-one-year-old Brendon Taylor had helped Zimbabwe overwhelm the all-weather champs and weren't India on a roll?

On the day of the Australia game, Kingsmead once again highlighted the melting pot of creeds and colours T20 had managed to cobble together. I remember Chris and Roberta, a unique couple—Chris, an Australian settled in South Africa who had never managed to reconcile himself to the fact; Roberta, an Indian born in Gujarat. Both were supporting Australia. As Roberta explained, 'I'm doing it for Chris, and him only.' The youngest of their two sons, all of ten, seemed the most passionate cricket supporter, yelling out 'South Africa' every time the words 'India' or 'Dhoni' were uttered! They had never been together to a cricket game before. Sitting across them were three Indian brothers, each holding a separate flag, one rooting for India, the other dressed in Aussie colours, the third a grumpy looking South African fan, the eldest, who had arranged to bring them all together!

I remember spotting the beaming Steve Elworthy, the former South African pacer who was director of the tournament, allowing himself a moment of self-congratulation. 'I wasn't half as famous as a player, but the tournament is ending and I'm sad,' he declared gleefully. He said the cheapest ticket, at R20 cheaper than the flags, caps and T-shirts selling at the stands, had made the difference. 'That, of course, and the cheap beer,' he winked. He was the first to say that the success of the tournament would lay to rest FIFA's fears ahead of South Africa hosting the 2010 soccer World Cup.

India, as it were, managed to go past the Aussie pacers, with Yuvraj Singh, all divine timing and devilish brutishness, making the difference with a well-made 70 after returning from an elbow injury. The dark horses were now top dogs. MS Dhoni experimented with a risky formula he was to try again in the final, that of giving Joginder Sharma the last over. Hayden and Symonds were running away with the game but first Sreesanth and then Harbhajan turned things around. Every time the Aussies looked like pulling it away, India pulled it back.

Pakistan had already beaten New Zealand and life stopped in India, and elsewhere, as the India-Australia match was on. A flight to London, due to take off at 1 a.m., was held back because the passengers begged and pleaded for the match to end. Nothing else mattered on Indian television screens, creating the kind of hysteria even the IPL's success failed to match in subsequent years. Things weren't that much different in South Africa, where local loyalties had shifted camp to India following the home team's exit. At the end of the game, I bumped into Roberta and family trying to look for a quick exit amid the throng and she solemnly declared there weren't any nails left to chew!

A word about Pakistan, who had declared during the 'bowlout' that they struggled to remember the rules of the tournament. The short and sweet nature of the tournament suited their natural flair and temperament well. Shahid Afridi came of age as a bowler. Whichever team could hold their nerve better in the final would win and here India had an edge. Dhoni, already getting into his groove as captain, famously declared ahead of the Indo-Pak final, 'The less we think, the better.'

On the day of the final, the crowds nearly caused a stampede at the Bullring. A ponytailed Shah Rukh Khan, later to own an IPL team, came out every few minutes on the balcony to smoke and everything went haywire. Everyone was surprised: so many South Africans turned up. The beer flowed. But once the game began, Shah Rukh could enjoy his smoke breaks in peace. There were other heroes to watch.

Events preceding the final also highlighted the dark side of such euphoria. The millionaire Allen Stanford cleverly chose the platform to launch his Stanford T20 initiative in the West Indies, and Vivian Richards and some other West Indies greats tagged along with him, blissfully unaware of future pitfalls and Stanford's jail term. Viv declared that he could hardly believe a tournament without Sachin Tendulkar had captured the public imagination and lauded Dhoni's team for playing with 'freshness and belief'. Those were the days of innocent T20 fever, and talk of moneybags were best left to a later date. For the moment, Elworthy's promise of cheap tickets had gone for a toss. Tickets worth R160 were selling for R1000.

The final was probably the best ever in an ICC tournament since 1975 and I'm not exaggerating one bit, even given the later exploits of MS Dhoni's team in winning a World Cup at home. That final, and the one we are talking about, had a common hero in Gautam Gambhir, who was assured before the tournament that he would have his place as opening bat in the XI, no matter what. The faith was repaid in full. He completed 200 runs in the tournament in the final, finally getting out for seventy-five, the highest ever by any Indian batsman in T20 at that point. Some lusty hitting by Rohit Sharma got India to 157, batting first. Imran Nazir was threatening to run away with the game till Robin Uthappa's direct throw irrevocably altered the course.

Pakistan seemed to be running away with the chase but India pulled it back again until it seemed only Misbah's resistance remained. With three wickets in hand they needed fifty-four runs from twenty-four balls but Misbah hit Harbhajan for three sixes and Sohail Tanveer somehow managed to race to twelve from four balls. With Pakistan needing thirteen off the final over with only one wicket left, Dhoni handed the ball to Joginder again.

Misbah hit a six and it all seemed over for India. Then he got too cute and repeated his Durban failing: a scoop ballooned to Sreesanth at short fine leg. An eternity of a moment later, it was finally over. Sreesanth held on. India won their first World Cup since 1983. The Boys in Blue turned men before our eyes. All hell and heaven broke loose.

The calculative MS Dhoni, for probably the only time in his career, lost his poise, forgetting the loss to New Zealand and declaring that India had remained unbeaten throughout the tournament. The BCCI announced a $3 million reward and a special prize running into a crore for Yuvraj alone. Young India, with a squad of an average age of twenty-five, made its mark.

In hindsight, there were a number of important observations. India bucked the trend and batted first after winning the toss. Dhoni's changes made up for the lack of a fifth bowler. With the hindsight of four IPLs behind us, we know now what Dhoni said then was brilliant observation: That, with wickets in hand, two runs per ball in the last eight overs were a possibility. Dhoni also declared, in the same breath, that T20 performances were no yardstick for selection into Test teams. The tournament belonged to the bowlers. Irfan Pathan was man of the match in the final, elbowing out Umar Gul. Shahid Afridi's leg-breaks earned him the man of the tournament award. Daniel Vettori had impressed, too.

Amid the haze of confetti, it was time for me to fly back. I had a long stopover in Mumbai, but I went out into the city and caught only traffic snarls and a brief glimpse of a parade, an open-top bus parade the likes of which are unlikely to be seen again.

Like I said, there are moments which are monsters. Such moments redefine a sport, stretch the boundaries of the probable and move nations. When you find yourself bang in the middle of it, it's unforgettable.

Journalists, athletes and fans wait for such moments.

But I had a flight to catch and rush back. For some reason which escapes me, I began to rummage through my rucksack, maybe because I was hungry and there was a bar of chocolate in there somewhere. Suddenly there it was, crisp and pristine, the ICC accreditation card which I had given up for lost, right next to the replacement. I could have sworn it wasn't there even a day ago.

Ah well, I had had two tickets all along to one of the grandest rides in Indian cricket and the birth of a new era. T20 had spoken and for the moment its word was gospel.

Postscript

This was the big bang. India's World Cup win in 2007—highlights of which are still regular staple on Indian sports television channels—spawned a mushrooming, multi-million dollar enterprise based around T20 cricket, changing the face of a traditional game which prizes patience as a virtue. To paraphrase Andy Warhol, in the future every cricketer will be famous for fifteen minutes, thanks to tournaments like the IPL, their celebrity owners and Bollywood packaging. On the flip side, four seasons into their blossoming romance with T20, India's cricket-crazy millions have discovered that their Test fortunes are dipping, their players tired and jaded, and the technique of their batsmen questionable. Is it all related? That's a story for another time!

Partha Bhaduri is Assistant Editor (Sports) with *The Times of India.* He has been writing about cricket for more than a decade, highlighting the complexities and nuances of a game inextricably woven into the fabric of Indian society.

Rukka's Minnesota Man

Shantanu Guha Ray

[For the girls in this impoverished tribal land, where villagers fix fireflies in cowdung to light their homes and live on frugal meals, Gastler is the God of Small Things.]

Village Rukka lies close to Ranchi, the capital of India's tribal Jharkhand state. Ranchi was once known as the home to India's largest mental asylum. Later it became synonymous with the Indian cricket captain, Mahendra Singh Dhoni, who shaped his cricket in this small, dusty town.

Though approachable by motorable roads, very few frequent Rukka village. There are some who carry on their bicycles coal mined from illegal pits. The village falls on their way to Ranchi. No wonder, then, that the village has not grown in economy, its two, big cemented structures being a government-run school and a guest house built by Usha Martin, a mining company high on iron ore and steel operations.

But every morning, the dusty grounds of this nondescript village reverberates as if soldiers are on a battle cry. In near-total darkness, young girl footballers move noisily to complete their mandatory jog before starting their day's practice. You have to stand close to watch them. They cannot be spotted from a distance because the village has no electricity, though it has lamp posts.

Leading the pack is a frail figure from faraway Minnesota, the US bread basket, who has made this obscure hamlet his home for more than five years. If spotted during the day, casual bystanders in Ranchi could mistake Franz Gastler as an Arcelor-Mittal representative prospecting for mines in this mineral-rich state. But for that, Gastler would have to wear an Armani suit and carry a camel leather bag for his laptop. He does none of that. He wears Adidas joggers, locally produced T-shirts and shorts and always joins the girls in their jogging routine.

For the girls in this impoverished tribal land, where villagers fix fireflies in cowdung to light their homes and live on frugal meals, Gastler is the God of Small Things. The twenty-seven-year-old Harvard graduate, who once served the finance ministry of the Columbian government in Bogota, pushed files and chewed pencils while working for the Boston Consulting Group (BCG) and is a trained ice hockey player, has—almost single-handedly—shaped the girls into a crack football unit.

This is no mean task in a state where no one shapes an agenda for girls. They are meant to be married off once they attain puberty. But Gastler has managed to change the mindset of the villagers and convinced them to send their daughters for a game of football. Besides fitness, the game would also open up a new world for the girls, Gastler argued for over a year before the rigid villagers were convinced.

In 2009, Jharkhand's Under-13 girl's football team—in just seven months—gained the fourth spot in national rankings from an abysmal twentieth and Gastler had seven of his girls in the side.

For a village where girls are routinely confined to the rigours of the kitchen and married during their schooling period, Gastler's achievement is incredible. The state's then chief minister, Shibu Soren, who once felt Gastler was a missionary on the prowl to convert and often made him sit outside his office for hours, loved him after his office bearers apprised him about Gastler's actual mission.

The office bearers also told Soren that football was a good way for the CM to show he was a man of the people. Soren jumped at the idea and allowed Gastler to train the girls. Soren, no longer the CM, feels Jharkhand could do with a few more Gastlers. The state's sports minister, Sudesh Mahato, calls him the Messi (read messiah) of Ranchi who lives with a popularity that has grown exponentially.

Yet, a humble Gastler says he did nothing and merely uncorked a fizzy bottle of soda. 'I was a mere connector. Let me be honest in telling you that the girls had tremendous potential, football was a rallying point and I merely connected the two. And everything worked very well for us,' says Gastler, who won his biggest battle in 2009 when—after years of persuasion—the parents allowed the girls to play football. 'That was tough. Often, I would return home in utter sadness. It was sacrilege for the parents to let their girls play football. Many almost picked up their machetes to hit me when I said the girls would have to train in the early morning hours.'

He won the first battle and got the girls out in the open, in the field and started their training sessions. At times, lack of facilities would hamper progress. It increased his frustration but also made Gastler realistic about what he had at his disposal: impoverished girls, second-hand equipment. 'The girls would have shaped well if there was some state support. You need coaches, fitness trainers and all of that. This is not cricket. India does not sway to football,' he adds. Yet, he was happy to have made a difference in the lives of the girls and continued his training with dogged determination.

Gastler knew that the change in the lives of the girls would not happen by chance. He remembers how he made his entry into Rukka.

Gastler, armed with support from BK Jhawar, former chairman of Usha Martin, walked into this village in early 2009 as a social worker keen to teach English in a school run by Khushi Gram Vikas Kendra (KGVK), a local NGO backed by Jhawar.

The steel baron also shielded him from initial criticism that, at times, was personal and made things extremely difficult for the American. Some dismissed the idea as a pie in the sky. A few bigots labelled him a missionary on the prowl while the village headman simply told him to shut up and leave. But slowly, the opposition faded when villagers saw—for themselves—Gastler's obsessions and the way he learnt to neutralise negative comments.

'Sahib worked very hard. He would be with us, day in and day out, working in the farms and in the school,' says Charku Mahato, a daily wage labourer who along with his wife—the village's only rice-beer (*haria*) seller—changed their mind after seeing Gastler ploughing an uneven field with a borrowed tractor and wiping out his entire savings to buy the girls football gear. Their only daughter, Sita Kumari, is a member of the state Under-13 squad, has immense potential and is known for her powerful volleys that beat seasoned goalkeepers hands down.

Seeing his daughter shape up well, Mahato joined Gastler in asking other villagers to let their daughters play football. The additional bonus was free education at the local school. The list, which started with just three footballers, is now brimming at 100 plus. Gastler calls it reverse social mobility.

Geeta, Sita and Neeta, regulars in the Jharkhand Under-13 squad, do not miss even one day of practice. In fact, playing football has made them supremely fit to handle household chores that include fetching water from the community bore pump and helping parents (read: mother) run errands in the kitchen.

'We cannot sleep before a special match,' says Sita. She recalls the 8-1 win over girls from New Delhi at the last nationals a moment to cherish. 'They all listened to music from their handsets and came to play the match in cars. We had one transistor for eighteen of us and slept on the floor,' says Sita, who has specialised in scissor kicks and rainbow headers. 'The Delhi goalkeeper didn't know what struck her. Probably her coach did not tell her that footballers can also score without facing the goal,' she laughs, remembering one of her goals.

Standing close, her friends nod in unison. For them, and their family, the game of football has been a great leveller.

'We are convinced of making it to the junior team. And if he (Gastler) stays with us, we are sure to give the national team many wonderful moments, we just have to wait till that happens,' says Neeta Murmu.

For Gastler, it is almost like writing his own history, penning his own biography. 'I am isolating myself from everything with a dedicated focus to get the girls to play and perform on the pitch. I will win if they win.'

Gastler also knows his disadvantages. He has not rocked world football with some memorable performances. Nor is he a trained coach with a degree from FIFA, the game's controlling body. Worse, he has to raise over ₹20 lakh to keep the team going every year. And he wants to take his job seriously and not as an assignment of casual amusement.

Some help is coming. The state government could open some cash doors for Gastler, who has also been promised funding by Coca-Cola India, sponsors of the Mir Iqbal Trophy for juniors. 'We are happy that he is working at the grass-roots level. This is encouraging news for us because we are keen to promote soccer at the junior level,' says the corporate affairs head of Coca-Cola India.

But the task is tough and Herculean.

At times, he misses cosmopolitan Minnesota, vibrant New York and days in the Indian capital where he learnt his first skills in football while dodging pesky cycle rickshaw drivers during a morning jog. He often misses Carlsberg beer and Subway sandwiches but once he sits down under the open sky for a frugal meal with the parents of the girls, he is at peace with himself.

'No one doubts him in the village. Once he was a foreigner who was viewed with caution. Now he is not a foreigner, he is an Indian. He is the first person to go to the ground for practice. He goes there at 4:30 a.m., when it's still dark. Only the village dogs give him company. And then, we all reach,' says John Toppo, one of the coaches of the side, talking of Gastler's no-nonsense football regime.

Toppo hasn't trained professionally but knows how to dribble and score goals with 40-yard cannonball drives. During training with Gastler and the girls, he focuses on what he calls precision training that involves getting two girls to play one-on-one to bypass a wall of defenders.

'I am no Alex Ferguson but I know it's important for footballers to be fleet-footed to hoodwink the defenders,' adds Toppo, who makes no apologies for his defensive style of goal-stopping game. His plan is to use counter-attacks. 'One of those counter-attacks is enough to win us the game.' Nearby, Gastler fixes bamboo poles to create the makeshift goalposts.

Football is working for all. Such is the magical pull of the game that when Poonam Toppo got engaged, she insisted Gastler talk to the boy and make him understand that playing football was more important than kneading flour every evening in the kitchen.

Strangely the boy, Rajesh Oraon, agreed. 'I will not pull her off the pitch. If that's what satisfies her, I have no problem. She should continue playing football,' Oraon said during a casual visit to his would-be wife's home. Sitting nearby on a wooden plank, Gastler agreed that it was a big call in rural India.

'We should build a home for him here,' says Savitri, the mother of Sita Kumari. There are times when she is embarrassed seeing Gastler at her home in the evening, crowded with beer drinkers who pay ₹10 for an earthen pot of *haria* and another ten rupees for a cup of peanuts. 'He is God for my daughter, he inspired her. Without him, she would be working with me in the kitchen, making *haria* for the villagers. That would be a life of obscurity. He has helped my daughter understand life and shaped her future. We are ever grateful to him,' adds Savitri.

Gastler, standing close, is saying nothing about his future. He is, in fact, already talking about Jharkhand's chances of reaching the finals of the next Under-13 tournament and even winning the trophy.

Today is his happiest day. The girls will play their first match under the floodlights of a huge stadium in the heart of Ranchi. The sanction came after days and weeks of deliberations and countless visits to the state bureaucrats. But what if the lights snap, a routine occurrence in Ranchi? Gastler laughs. He has asked many of his wealthier friends in the city to carry their handsets. But that would be just flickers in the dark?

Gastler laughs the loudest. He is used to fireflies and knows how to take advantage of their glow. 'The light and the limelight will remain forever.' No one disputes his verdict in Rukka.

Postscript

No one in Ranchi calls him an American monk on the prowl anymore. No one blames him for trying to woo the town's gullible tribal folk with images of Christ and cash. Instead, Franz Gastler, the trained management graduate from the United States who has made Rukka village his permanent home, is now popular as Franz Sahib. His four-year-old plus work is paying off: Nike and Coca-Cola are already chipping in with funds for an academy and a girls' football league. The girls, all trained by Gastler, are going places. One represents India U-15 team while three are in India U-13 team. And their parents are not pushing them for marriage, nor do they do menial labour in the farmlands. They just study and kick around throughout the day. Gastler has not picked up any awards from the state government or the Indian sports minister who works out of the Indian capital, far away from the dusty hamlet where Gastler works tirelessly. Gastler is not worried: his awards are the smiles of the girls. And fireflies that the villagers fix in cow dung every night to light their homes.

Shantanu Guha Ray has spent over two decades in journalism specialising in both sports and business, his last assignment was as Deputy Editor, *India Today*. His maiden book, a biography of Mahendra Singh Dhoni, the Indian cricket captain, will soon hit the stands. He is currently working on his next book, *The Great Indian Newsroom Madness*.

That Tragic November Day of 1982

S Thyagarajan

> The mood in the galleries was one of unbridled elation. The frenzy of joy spreading around was extraordinary. How one wished it remained that way! But, astonishingly, everything went topsy-turvy before you could pronounce Jack Robinson.

Is nostalgia a disease? Or is it an introspection that prompts a wave of memories, pleasant or otherwise?

I am at a loss to define it even as I wade back into the labyrinth of the past. It is an experience, the antithesis of exhilaration. It was, admittedly, traumatic, tragic in more than one sense of the word and truly a moment that destroyed the image and identity of an ethos cherished for decades.

What happened on that November afternoon in New Delhi amidst the cornucopia of expectations from millions is difficult to portray in words. This was the moment the whole country, the hockey fraternity across the globe, was waiting for amidst the fever and fervour of speculation.

The mood among the congregation of thousands braving the November chill and the scrutiny of an unprecedented scale of security at the National Stadium was understandable. It was buoyant, vibrant and vociferous.

For a journalist covering his first Asian Games, it was a moment compelling to soak in. I trudged my way early enough—three hours before the scheduled final—carrying a rickety Olivetti typewriter, to escape the rigours of the security drill into the media box. The distance to the scene of action at the National Stadium was an irritant.

Suddenly, I realised there were already some people in the gallery adjacent to the VIP tribune. For a moment, I was stunned. There he was in his famous fur cap and dark glasses; he was none other than the chief minister of my state, Tamil Nadu, the charismatic MGR. He was at the opening ceremony with J Jayalalitha. The pair was probably the most photographed duo during the opening ceremony.

I am bringing this out merely to underscore the interest generated by the Asian Games, the second India was hosting after 1951, at the same venue—the National Stadium. More importantly, for everyone on that day, it was also a theatre for the battle of the decade—the gold medal clash between India and Pakistan.

I cherish even today the few moments I shared with MGR before the final. Taking an enormous risk, I crossed over the low barricade to wish the CM. After a formal greeting and presenting my credentials as the accredited journalist for the games from *The Hindu*, a newspaper MGR cared for and whose content and truth-telling he respected, the conversation perforce centred on India's chances of capturing the gold after a sixteen-year old hiatus after that momentous final in Bangkok in 1966.

MGR wanted to know whether the Indian team was strong enough for the task ahead and sought my judgement on it. 'Your understanding about the calibre of the teams must be better than mine,' he observed.

Not letting go an opportunity to show off my expertise, which was governed more by patriotism than pragmatism, I vouched that India enjoyed the home advantage apart from a splendid record in the previous matches. And also, I added that Pakistanis had to reckon with the huge crowd factor.

By the time I could indulge further by sitting next to the CM—that would have been impossible in my home city—in came a handsome young man answering by the name of Rajiv Gandhi.

As the helmsman who played a prominent role in the conduct of the games, Rajiv was surprised to see MGR seated in a gallery that was not part of the VIP enclosure.

When Rajiv implored MGR to move into the VIP area, MGR was a tad reluctant and even a bit embarrassed by the attention. But Rajiv would have nothing of it. He put his arms around him and gently pulled him out of the seat. MGR could resist no further.

As excitement mounted across the ground with spectators surging in, searching for a vantage viewing point in that vast stadium, the cynosure no doubt was the prime minister, Indira Gandhi. She was the key figure behind India staging the games after the earlier government had shown a marked dislike to meet the enormous expenditure the planners envisaged.

The personal interest she evinced in seeing the games through, to enhance the country's reputation and image, was commendable. How proud was this gracious lady when she presented the first gold medal of the games to India's Raghubir Singh in equestrian.

It is not easy to surmise now what Indira Gandhi's thoughts were as she occupied the seat. Was she dreaming of decorating the

Indian players on the podium with a gold medal around their necks? Was she imagining the message that an Indian victory would send to the neighbours across the border, and, quite conceivably, across the continent or the world at large? I keep thinking about this even today.

Even after nearly four decades, the visage of the National Stadium overflowing with crowds remains etched in memory. The enthusiasm and excitement were escalating by the minute to a feverish pitch. The anticipation for the start was frenetic.

Journalists in the media box were edgy, debating the pros and cons, weighing the strengths and weaknesses. But caution was an underlying sentiment. 'It is not easy to predict the verdict in an India-Pakistan final, or for that matter in any match and at any level,' opined a senior scribe from a popular New Delhi newspaper. As a widely travelled journalist with a few Olympics finals under his belt, his observation was acknowledged without a murmur.

What many of us thought put India ahead of Pakistan was the sequence of victories in the earlier rounds. Until the semi-final, India had conceded just one goal to Malaysia in the opening match (5-1). A 10-0 result against Oman and a dozen over Bangladesh generated predictable euphoria. The 7-2 swamp against Japan was taken as an authoritative signal before the final verdict.

The record for Pakistan was somewhat similar. The team had conceded one goal to Japan before the semi-final. The verdict against Malaysia in the penultimate round match was a wee bit disconcerting for Pakistan. A 2-0 result against the overwhelming margin for India against Japan clearly shoved the home team into the spot as the favourite.

'Even a soothsayer will hesitate to pick the winner of the India-Pakistan contest for the hockey gold. However, the record and form of the team provide a few pointers…there can be no two opinions that India has won its matches with a greater measure of comfort than Pakistan,' I wrote as the initial paragraph in my pre-final assessment. And the enthusiastic sub-editor on *The Hindu* sports desk coined an optimistic heading, 'Form book favours India'.

Little did anyone of us realise that a catastrophic verdict was in the offing. The ball began to roll and India gained an early lead from a penalty stroke that germinated following a rattling raid involving Mohammed Shahid and Merwyn Fernandez.

The thrust and skill demonstrated by the duo simply bewildered the hesitant goalkeeper Shahid Ali Khan to go for a desperate bid to cut the move. When M Clark, the Kiwi umpire, showed the spot, the remonstration by the Pakistanis to the ruling looked somewhat comical and decidedly out of place. Zafar Iqbal, skipper, slotted in the lead without a trace of emotion.

The mood in the galleries was one of unbridled elation. The frenzy of joy spreading around was extraordinary. How one wished it remained that way! But, astonishingly, everything went topsy-turvy before you could pronounce Jack Robinson.

Unpredictability may be the essence of life. And sport is no exception. But the transformation we witnessed on that mellowing evening was stunning, leaving everybody speechless. Unbelievable!

India was hurtling towards a defeat that eventually turned out to be unprecedented, unexpected and utterly morale-shattering. I still shudder to think that such a thing had really occurred, India losing 1-7, a final before the home crowd and in front of the dignitaries headed by none other than the Iron Lady, Indira Gandhi.

Amidst all the chaos and the pandemonium on the field where a goal glut erupted, leaving a hapless Mir Ranjan Negi to pay for the sins of the defenders and attackers, I could not resist a creeping admiration for the Pakistanis, for their temperament, pugnacity and fortitude. Supporters for them were a clear minority, a small group of officials presided over by their dynamic president, Air Marshal Nur Khan.

'By no stretch of imagination should it be presumed that Pakistan dazzled. Almost throughout one missed the flair that had made Pakistan an outfit to be respected and feared. The equaliser and the lead that Pakistan obtained were an occurrence more than by design, but the confidence they generated underlined the further part of the drama and the concomitant pathos,' I wrote in *The Hindu*.

When the teams trooped in after the ceremonial introduction to the president, Giani Zail Singh, a topic that engaged the media was the inclusion of Syed Ali in preference to Jagdeep Singh. Somehow we felt that the move did not click. And sure enough, Syed Ali rendered the frontline less cohesive than what one noticed with Jagdeep Singh in the earlier matches.

Syed was replaced by Jagdeep midway but the move came about when the Indians were being submerged in a cascade of moves by Kalimullah and Samiullah, with Hassan Sardar and Hanif Khan constructing their own routes to the goal.

But here I do not intend to grow wiser after the event. When I recall the mood of consternation in the media box—I was also partly struck by that reality—precious little was achieved by the substitution, as the result eventually exhibited.

In a one-to-one comparison the proficiency level of the Pakistan players was clearly on the higher side. There was none in the Indian attack to match the class and calibre of Hassan Sardar. Unquestionably, he was the hero. For the Pakistanis he was a reincarnation of Dhyan Chand.

In fact, many Pakistani commentators like Munir Dar were convinced that Hassan Sardar during the 1980s was a shade better even than the incomparable Dhyan Chand! They cited their own reasons, though unacceptable to me, for such an assumption.

The wingers Kalimullah and Samiullah were truly world class as was Hanif Khan, whose incisive moves were a treat to behold. The Pakistani defenders Manzur and Qasim Zia shielded their goalkeeper Shahid Ali Khan more vigorously than Rajinder Singh, Vineet Kumar and Manohar Topno did for Negi. The Indian mid-field, save for a brave display by MM Somayya in parts, was anything but distinguishable. In fact, it began disintegrating after the equaliser was accomplished and at one point of time became invisible.

Minute by minute shouts of 'Pakistan Zindabad' and 'Allah Ho Akbar' rose to a crescendo. The Indian supporters stood stupefied, unable to digest the fact that their hopes were slithering down the abyss of despair. Tears and jeers were all that they managed to generate as it was becoming clearer that India was being consigned to the dust of defeat.

As a sum up, I noted in my dispatch, 'The anguish can well be imagined. The ignominy of the show will haunt enthusiasts for a long time to come. The Indian team belied all expectations it produced by the runaway victories in the earlier matches. To blame an individual for the defeat in a team game is uncharitable; but the name of the goalkeeper, Mir Ranjan Negi, will figure prominently as the cause for this defeat.'

A pensive Indira Gandhi sat through the concluding proceedings. Her inner anguish could not be fathomed but she looked sombre, dismayed perhaps by a melancholic wrap up. Everyone was sure the prime minister would present the medals; but when we saw Muhammad Hidyatullah, vice-president, performing that task it was clear how disappointed Indira Gandhi must have been at the horror she was subjected to watch.

To say the prize distribution ceremony had the veneer of a funeral is no exaggeration. The crowds had begun to disperse long before the podium got ready. Actually, not many were willing to witness the Pakistanis dancing in delight with the gold medals glittering on their chests. Misplaced patriotism, or a show of regret? I wondered whether we lacked the civility to give the winners their due respect and commendation, even if it was not so spontaneous.

A blanket of silence enveloped the National Stadium, reflecting the mood of the nation. I had a strange feeling of emptiness. Somehow the spirit had gone, or evaporated, by the sequence of events that I was totally unprepared to encounter.

A reverse would not have impacted me so much as the margin and the enormity of the dent on the reputation and history of the country in hockey. What a humiliation it was for a seasoned coach like Balbir Singh (Sr), who had savoured the joy of winning three Olympic Gold medals, the third medal won at Melbourne in 1956 under his stewardship.

Gracious and graceful as ever, Balbir Singh, managing to look unperturbed, acknowledged the verdict in a philosophical, it-was-not-our-day, refrain. But it was not difficult to perceive the inner turbulence of suffering the ignominy of a huge reverse before an unprecedented turnout waiting to give the team a tumultuous ovation.

However, much as I struggled to shrug off the effect of the result on my person, I was unsuccessful. As the hours passed, and even long after the closing ceremony, when I prepared to take the train back home, there was an inexplicable remorse that lingered. It persists even today and whenever a reference is made of that final match, a chill courses through my veins.

But why, I ask myself repeatedly and sometimes in a state of exasperation, does a defeat against Pakistan become unacceptable even when conceding the fact that the opponent was better equipped in many sectors? I am not referring here to the verdict at the New Delhi Asian Games alone.

There have been several well-contested encounters where India proved decidedly superior, like the Champions Trophy in Amsterdam in 2003. The recovery after everything had gone awry ranks, to my mind, as one of the best-ever combat against the Pakistanis.

What amazes me is the degree of consistency, if not efficiency, that the Pakistanis have managed to bring into the matches against India. From the Pakistani perspective it is, quite palpably, a question of prestige. A win against the much clichéd 'traditional opponent' is a reflection of a national sentiment, an emotionally fulfilling moment to conquer the biggest neighbour.

What welds a Pakistani team into a thunderstorm when India is the opponent? Is it passion, or pride or religion? Can it be a combination of all the three factors? Such puzzling posers always haunt me, and continue to do so.

As one of the few journalists who have seen the best of both the teams here and across the border, apart from in various other climes and venues, I am yet to convince myself of what separates India and Pakistan in the field of hockey.

The players on both sides are the first to concede that any contest between the two is a toss-up. No one wagers on the outcome with a degree of certainty. And that perhaps underlines the unpredictability of hockey, even in these days of match-fixing.

An India-Pakistan encounter fulfils the senses because of its unfolding touch of aesthetics. For all the corruption in the system that has become a fashion to debate, style and skill levels, not to speak of the periodical changes in rules, the element of classicism continues to hold sway. The viewership for an India-Pakistan encounter is still rated as the highest in international hockey.

Pakistan today may not have an artiste of the calibre of a Hassan Sardar or a Samiullah or, for India, anyone in the mould of a Zafar Iqbal, a Shahid or a Merwyn Fernandez of that era, but the verve and vibrancy that pleases a connoisseur is yet to become a relic in the vortex of power hockey, or total hockey, or whatever fancy name you give to portray today's approach.

We have come a long, long way after the Asian Games final of 1982. A revolution has swept the sport, eliminating chunks of its character, stripping it of the essential element—artistry. Neither Pakistan nor India was prepared for this eventuality. Both countries have been outpaced, out-manoeuvred and outgrown by a new emerging power equation, the balance shifting towards Europe.

That November of 1982 may be a dead-letter today, having little or no relevance to contemporary hockey, governed by a set of totally incomprehensible laws and comical conditions of play to suit the whims and fancies of the gallery occupiers. A generous measure of goals is all that matters today.

But for the generation that turned up for the memorable gold medal final in 1982, all that mattered was how well a goal could be conceived and completed. For them, hockey was an amalgam of a serenade and symphony, where skill and style triumphed over the rigidity of a system rather than power and precision prevailing over the combination of artistry, athleticism and adroitness.

As memories of that disaster against Pakistan sink slowly without an administered balm of amnesia, I am at a loss to estimate how long the nation will suffer from this hurt to its psyche. Will there be a chance for India to pay back Pakistan in the same coin in any of the Asian Games that are to follow? Until that happens, it would be impossible to obliterate the horrors of the defeat from memory for decades to come. Will that day ever dawn at all?

Postscript

The Delhi disaster triggered a snowballing debacle. The impact is felt even today. India went tumbling down the pedestal, unable to accomplish anything noteworthy; the only silver lining was the gold medal triumph in the 1998

Bangkok Asian Games. Triumphs, not exceptional though by international standards, in the Azlan Shah Cup and Prime Minister's Gold Cup at Dhaka and the Asian Champions trophy at Ordos, spread a modicum of fragrance. But the decline in every aspect has been perceptible. This was contributed largely by inept, inert and irresponsible administrators who have jostled for power but proved incompetent when it came to performance. The growth was stifled by constant shuffling of players; coaches; poor, unimaginative programming; inadequate wherewithal and lack of dynamism in every area. The trials and tribulations are well exemplified by the last place in the World Cup of 1986 in England. What haunts still is the failure to make the grade for the Olympics in Beijing in 2008, and, of course, the intractable imbroglio in the administration since then.

S Thyagarajan has been covering hockey for *The Hindu* since 1967. He has covered six Olympics (1984-2004), eight World Championships (1982-2010), eight Asian Games (1982-2010), and six Asian Championships (1985-2007).

He has been a member of the Communications Committee in the International Hockey Federation since 1998. He was the chairman of Field Hockey Commission, Association Internationale De La Press Sportive (1998-2006). At present, he is the chairman of the Media Commission in the Asian Hockey Federation.

Perfection is not a Chimera

Kamesh Srinivasan

> Abhinav Bindra has graduated from being a world champion to an Olympic champion. To own those two crowns at the same time was a rarity in the world of sport. There was nothing left to achieve!

It was the launch of his book *A Shot at History*. Abhinav Bindra was quite relaxed, not too worried about how the book would fare in the market. He was pleased he had done his bit, to tell the world how the first individual Olympic gold was won by an Indian, a small drop in an ocean of billions. It was for the young generation to get inspired from his example, his story.

Writing a book was a thankless job. He was not doing it for the money. There was none. He was willing to share his journey with the world, even as he was attempting to chart a new course. He had no secrets to tell except a graphic account of the hard road to success, littered with uncertainties.

The only guarantee, he realised soon in his career, was that there were no guarantees for success. You may leave little to chance, but it may be a matter of chance that everything would fall in place at the moment of reckoning. His story may be intimidating for many, for he pursued perfection relentlessly for more than a decade, locking himself in solitary confinement at his private range forever, punching holes in a black paper, from 10 metres. Literally, he was a monk in meditation. He was quick to point out that there were many roads to Rome. He chose the most difficult, perhaps because it suited his temperament.

What worked for him may not suit another person, but all the same it was important to present his story, so that people understood what mattered was the desire to achieve. You fulfil your heart's desire only when you forget the target and focus purely on the path. The target should be in the background, merely fuelling the fire, whereas you think only about the process and not the goal.

Indian sports had been unnerved by the magnitude of the goal, and had perhaps given up along the way, for over a hundred years. Abhinav himself was perplexed, when he reached the summit, as to how no other Indian had scaled that height before. Though it was his third attempt, he had accomplished the ultimate goal in sports when he was twenty-six.

If anything, Abhinav had used all the hurdles to lift himself to new heights. An intelligent man uses both his good and bad fortune to his advantage. Abhinav was quite smart to pick up the good points even from a bitter enemy and always kept an open mind for ideas.

'Just baby steps,' the World and Olympic champion responded when complimented on his silver medal in the Asian Air Gun championship in October 2011. The team had won the gold in men's air rifle, and Gagan Narang had finished seventh. It had been so different in the Asian Games in Guangzhou, China, in 2010. Gagan Narang had been gunning for the gold and was on par with the eventual gold medallist, Zhu Qinan of China, before the latter pulled ahead on the last two shots of the 10-shot final. Abhinav had failed to qualify for the final then, as he had faltered marginally in the shoot-off when he had tied with three others for the last two spots.

Well, it was unusual for Abhinav to finish ahead of Gagan. Even in the Commonwealth Games at home in Delhi, just prior to the Asian Games, Gagan had shot a world record 600 out of 600 on way to the gold, beating Abhinav by a big margin. Abhinav was happy with the silver then. He had no qualms about playing second fiddle to the Hyderabadi. For, he had nothing to prove to anyone after the Olympic gold. Quite honestly, nothing else had mattered to Abhinav in his young life.

That Olympic medal was the sole burning desire for the Chandigarh lad, ever since he decided to plunge into the world of 10-metre air rifle shooting under the mango tree in the backyard of his guru Colonel Jagir Singh Dhillon's home. Every competition was an experiment, even when he had to ensure qualification for the Olympics. Abhinav made it difficult for himself in those world level competitions by keeping unrealistic targets for himself, for he knew that he had to get used to every possible pressure situation so as to simulate the Olympic pressure, the ultimate challenge for a sportsman.

Of course, in the early days, when he was learning the tricks of the trade and trying to master his sport, both physically and mentally, it was a lot simpler for Abhinav, as he just wanted to improve. He had improved so much even when he was so young that he came close to making the Olympics final in Sydney in 2000. He missed it by one point. He was seventeen then and the youngest shooter in the Games.

He was good enough to shoot a world junior record of 596 out of 600 then in a World Cup, but not good enough to qualify for the Olympics. He needed a wild card entry, the 'hardship quota' as it was called, for Indian shooting itself was taking baby steps on the world stage. He was one of the bright prospects along with Anjali Bhagwat, who went on to make the women's air rifle final, on another 'wild card', in the Sydney Games.

He had watched the Olympics on television in 1992 and 1996. He was fascinated by the aura. He cultivated a dream and then chose his sport. He had tried a bit of everything and realised only golf rounds with his father over the weekends had given him any degree of success and happiness. He got glued to his gun soon and was quite talented to shoot the balloon kept on the head of his housemaid in the garden. He was sharp but the skill had to be honed over thousands of hours, over many years, to reach Olympic heights. He was game.

When he aimed a shot at glory in Athens, Greece, in 2004, Abhinav had done everything possible, or so he thought. His preparation was intense, his disappointment equally high following the debacle in the Athens Games, when he qualified for the final at No 3, then slid to No 7 after an unusually disastrous final round. Abhinav could not help becoming the world champion two years later in Zagreb, Croatia, in 2006. It was not part of his scheme!

Rajyavardhan Singh Rathore, the silver medallist in Athens in 2004, was very convincing when he said at the press conference for the medallists in the Greek capital that Abhinav would be a world champion one day. In a way, it was a normal observation about a person who lived his sport every single moment of his life. Rathore remarked about Abhinav, as a man in 'constant comatose'.

Abhinav had no excuses to offer, except that he had felt the floor unusually slippery at the range in Athens. He had released ten perfect shots. They had landed him the wrong scores. Something was amiss. He was categorical that he was still in the 'zone' after having shot 597 in qualification, an improvement on the Olympic record. He was not exhausted by the effort in the qualification.

It was a huge mystery for Abhinav and he had to swallow his pride and the ignominy of being labelled a 'chicken heart' who could not handle the pressure of an Olympic final. In fact, the situation had not overwhelmed him, he was as competent to handle the stage as the seasoned exponents. It was circumstances that robbed him of a medal. As was discovered by his coach Gaby Buehlmann of Switzerland, who had positioned his rifle and other equipment on lane three, the space below the wooden surface where he stood was hollow, leading to a bounce. When you are aiming to hit a pin's head from 10 metres, you need to freeze like a statue at the moment when you pull the trigger.

The officials could have ordered a rematch had the discrepancy been pointed out in time. But they found it only two days later, when Gaby was positioning another of her shooters, from Italy, on that same 'suspicious' lane three in that final range for eight shooters. It was some consolation for Abhinav eventually to know that it was not his fault and he had actually been robbed of a medal.

Abhinav was not too keen to tell the world the real story then, for nobody could get his medal back. He took in the experience, imbibing the lesson that you had control only in terms of execution, results were always a lottery. The bitter experience completely detached him from the goal. He started enjoying the pursuit and realised the need to live in the present, enjoying every small moment in the process. No point waiting for the ultimate glory to rejoice, for it may never happen. There were no guarantees for success.

Yet, he was only twenty-two. He was human, pulled hard by the emotions of the experience. He needed all the persuasive powers of his parents who backed him completely even when he had chosen the most unglamorous sport, and coaches Heinz Reinkemier and Uwe Riesterer, apart from Gaby and his mentor for many years from childhood, Amit Bhattacharjee, to put Abhinav back on the rail, in pursuit of his Olympic dream. He had lived a nightmare. It was not easy to wake up and be calm. Quite typical of his character, Abhinav learnt the lesson from the bitter experience and moved on.

He strengthened his preparation for the next Olympics. He did a lot more than before and went to the extent of undergoing commando training in Germany, pretty close to the Beijing Games, and got rid of the 'fear of failure' and the 'fear of the unknown', as he stood like a monk in meditation, on a 'pizza pole', many metres above the ground. He realised new pockets of untapped energy, reserves of mental fortitude that surfaced in time to salvage his pride. He knew that he could dig deep.

No wonder that Abhinav said, 'I have started believing in my beliefs, and doubting my doubts,' when queried about his preparation for the games, in one of his rare interviews a few days before the Beijing Games. He also said that he was 'proud' of his preparation, as he had done everything possible. Yes, he had even mapped his brain and tried to recreate the positive atmosphere when he could shoot the 10s, like a machine. He had also hoodwinked the Chinese, weeks in advance, to sell him their pellets that would fetch him the best score in the games!

It was thus a nightmare revisited when Abhinav shot 4.2 during the first of the 'sighter' shots in Beijing four years after Athens, in another Olympic final. He had never shot such a score even when he had picked up the rifle for the first time. It was always a fight between the 10s and the 9s. The rare '8', once during practice, shamed him so much that he hid the paper target away from the glare of his guru!

Destiny cannot be so cruel. He had given his life for the sport and pursued it with diligence and intelligence. He had improved so much he was ready to be decorated with a doctorate in 'air rifle shooting'. He had experimented with everything, from cutting his jacket to designing his own shooting shoes. He had learnt to shoot the 10s against the most irritating disturbances, specially simulated during practice, so that nothing could be a surprise for him anymore and shake his concentration.

Nobody could believe the score that blinked on the screen in August 2008, when Abhinav released the first 'sighter' shot in that limited sanctioned time of five minutes of final preparation before the final. The shooter had to get to a 'ready' position with his equipment, with unlimited 'sighter' shots.

After throwing a quick glance of desperation at his coach Gaby, Abhinav got down to setting the rifle straight. He gave a phenomenal number of 40-odd 'clicks' to get the alignment right. He had no time to think how the rifle had lost its setting, after having been set for the qualification series. It could have been an accident, it could have been a case of sabotage, as was reported by a section of the media, that tended to point a finger of suspicion on the coach of the Indian team, Laszlo Szucsak of Hungary, as he had been involved in a few unpleasant altercations with Abhinav in the run-up to the games.

Champions do not get lost in the negatives. They respond to moments like only champions can. Abhinav was ready in quick time. His first shot in the final was 10.7. He was ready to shake the world and reach his destination. He shot like a robot, as all the uncertainty had combined to give him such a rude shock before the final that he was tuned beautifully for execution without any emotion.

Despite conceding a two-point lead after the qualification series of sixty shots, to Henri Hakkinen of Finland, and a one-point lead to defending champion Zhu Qinan of China, Abhinav pulled on brilliantly with every shot, moving from the fourth position to take a 0.2 point lead after the seventh shot. His scores read 10.7, 10.3, 10.4, 10.5, 10.5, 10.5 and 10.6. His lead was reduced to 0.1 after the eighth shot when he came up with a 10.0. With a 10.2 on the ninth, he was tied for the gold with Hakkinen. It was then that Abhinav released the 'Brahmastra', the ultimate salvo, a quick 10.8 last shot, the first to hit the target among the eight shooters. It was tough to beat him after that.

In air rifle shooting, the last shot can often decide whether you have a medal or not. It is generally that close. You need to finish strong. Abhinav had shown his strength of finish in the world championship in Zagreb with a 10.7 last shot. He had trained himself to tackle the final. To shoot 104.5 in the Olympic final was a dream fare.

Thus, Abhinav Bindra graduated from being a world champion to an Olympic champion. To own those two crowns at the same time was a rarity in the world of sport. There was nothing left to achieve!

It is a pity he does not get the recognition for the unparalleled achievement in Indian sport. No wonder sport flounders in the country. Quite often, we do not understand and appreciate the deeds of our champions.

Naturally, after the initial euphoria of the triumph and all the celebration back home, when the whole country rejoiced like one person, there was a sense of emptiness in Abhinav, as he went through weird emotions and did not want to shoot a competition any more. Shooting was like breathing for Abhinav, he would continue with it, but no question of going through the 'torture' of competition any more. There was nothing left to prove.

He had climbed Mount Everest, and found 'nothing' there. He had sacrificed success along the way, as he had only two bronze medals in the numerous world cups over the years to show, to reach his ultimate goal of becoming the Olympic champion. Being a world champion was definitely not part of the scheme, as it was felt that it would make it that much more difficult for him to do it again in the

Olympic Games. You need to nurse the hunger and cannot afford to satiate it, on a big stage.

Abhinav proved that theory wrong.

He battled a severe back pain after becoming the world champion and even missed the Asian Games in Doha in 2006 to regain complete fitness. He jumped many hurdles to reach the Beijing Games.

Despite being a world champion and the man who had won the Olympic quota, there was no guarantee the national federation would select him to represent the country in the Olympic Games. The rules state that the quota is won for the country. Fine, but you can't overlook a world champion, who has been religiously preparing for a 'shot at glory', on the flimsy ground of current form. The tiger was crouching for a final leap.

Yet, there was a lot of agony when the head of the federation made a flippant remark that PT Raghunath would be a better bet in place of Abhinav, when the former was crowned the Asian champion. Gagan Narang, the other air rifle specialist, was shooting too well and was an automatic choice.

By his own admission, Abhinav had over the years taken advantage of the lack of a clear selection policy by the national federation, but the uncertainty was too much to bear. It was left to experts like Uwe Riesterer to keep him psychologically stable and focused on his task of concrete preparation. He had a point to prove, but he needed to be given a chance, in the first place.

Even when he shot a record 400 out of 400 in the Mavlankar Championship, the qualifying event for the National championship in 1996, the officials refused to believe him. He had already shot a perfect 600 in the Chandigarh state championship by then. Quite sensitive and thus sharply wounded, Abhinav vowed he would prove himself to all the doubters, some day.

From a precocious talent, Abhinav had become the world and Olympic champion. But it meant nothing when he tried to return to the sport, about two years after the Beijing Games. The authorities had become smart and drafted a selection policy that tended to ignore international achievements and gave considerable weight to the scores shot in national selection meets. There was a lot of miscommunication as the sports ministry tried to mediate and had no clue about what the national federation had planned in terms of trials and camps.

Abhinav realised he had to build a new road to Rome! He had to do it the 'chaotic Indian way' this time. His theories had to change. It was not an issue for him anymore. He was flexible. The new challenge would in fact enliven the passage for him.

It was thus no surprise that Abhinav started shooting the big scores in competitions that would not have mattered to him otherwise. He had to first ensure selection, though he had won the quota place in the fourth of five chances, at the World Cup in Germany. Abhinav had to keep a good average and needed to be in the top two in men's air rifle so that the authorities would not play with his selection for the London Games in 2012.

It was precisely for this reason that he completely outclassed the field, Gagan et al, in the National championship at Balewadi Complex in Pune in November 2011. After shooting 596, the same score that he had shot in the Beijing Games, Abhinav was close to his best, shooting a 104.2 in the final that saw him beat Gagan by a mile, 3.6 points to be precise. Maybe the latter was trying to keep a low profile and follow the path of India's first individual Olympic gold medallist, as he shot a 595, the same score that had tragically denied him a place in the Olympic final in Beijing.

Abhinav Bindra is ready to do it the 'chaotic Indian way'. Who knows, he may succeed this way as well. By his own admission he is working hard, and keeping things simple.

Postscript

Abhinav Bindra's disappointment at not picking up a medal in London was palpable. He won the gold in the Asian Shooting Championship in January 2012, with a fine last shot of 10.5 that saw him beat the reigning Asian Games champion and Athens Olympics gold medallist, Zhu Qinan of China, by 0.3 point. Bindra overcame a one-point deficit in the qualifying stage, and his total of 701.1 was 0.6 point better than his Olympic gold-winning fare. Yet after competing in three World Cups and training in Germany, the final in London was like a curtain descending on a brilliant career. Or do we see a resurrection in the months to come?

Kamesh Srinivasan works as a special correspondent with *The Hindu* newspaper. He has covered the Athens and Beijing Olympics, apart from the Doha and Guangzhou Asian Games. He has been covering sports, quite a variety of it, for more than twenty years. He studied in Chennai before moving to Delhi for work.

The Conquerors

Ayaz Memon

> 'It's the other way around,' said the Indian captain. 'Now they have to beat us.' He was obviously being hyperbolic but, in some ways, Kapil's seemingly off-the-cuff statement also reflected the mindset of the Indian players.

Show me a person who gave Kapil Dev's team any chance of winning the 1983 World Cup, and I will show you a liar and an opportunist.

The story of how David Frith, then editor of *Wisden Cricket Monthly*, had to literally eat his words after he wrote India off as no-hopers has been told far too often to be repeated here, yet is symbolic of the utter disdain with which the Indian cricket team was viewed before the tournament. To paraphrase Winston Churchill, the situation was 'hopeless, but not serious'.

I still recall the good-humoured immigration officer at Heathrow Airport, London, ribbing me when I told him I had come to cover the cricket. 'Are you serious?' he asked, which got me worried for a moment. Was there something wrong with my papers? Did this mean that I would be sent back home?

'You guys must be crazy about cricket, but you don't know how to play this limited over stuff at all,' he said, which put me at ease somewhat, but ill at ease too, if you get what I mean. I mean, India's record in the first two World Cups had been dismal, but did that have to be rubbed in every time?

To be honest, my own belief in the Indian team's prospects, too, tended towards zero. True, there had been some glimpses of excellence when Kapil Dev's team beat the mighty West Indies at Berbice in a one-day game preceding the 1983 tournament, but India's track record in one-day cricket was not something which could have set the Thames on fire.

So while I was obviously privileged to be covering a World Cup, on the nine-hour flight to England in May 1983 two issues jostled for pole position in my mind: Did I really want to give up law practice to pursue writing on cricket as a vocation? And, did it make any sense to watch India play West Indies at Old Trafford first up when I could watch England play New Zealand at the Oval?

By the time the plane landed at Heathrow, at least one issue had been resolved. The Oval it would be. This decision was not, as might be misconstrued, based on the kind of cynicism journalists are known to acquire over a period of time, or indeed the mild mocking of the immigration officer. I was on only my second overseas assignment, un-jaded and curious, but frankly, what logic lay in watching India play the best team in the world?

I have lived to regret that decision. Watching the young, classy, elegant Martin Crowe—touted as the next big thing in batsmanship—was a delightful experience in itself. But not seeing India floor the mighty West Indies at Old Trafford was such a bad miss that I was cheesed off and chastened.

The topsy-turvy nature of sport is something only the foolhardy can ignore. For instance, who would have thought Jimmy Connors would win Wimbledon in 1974, or that he would lose the final to veteran Arthur Ashe the following year when he was expected to win? The vicissitudes of sport—as in life—brook no linear logic. This lesson had been painfully learnt.

For the next month and more, I followed the Indian team diligently across the length and breadth of the country, spending long hours on British rail, making scores of trips on the London Underground, as the World Cup wound its way through that magnificent summer. The budget was modest, the travel itinerary intense but the experience was unbeatable—and there were other attractions an English summer offers, like catching a concert by Dire Straits at Earl's Court.

For the most, I stayed with a friend in Surbiton, Surrey. The place was way removed from the centre of London but had its attractions, not the least that it was only a couple of stations away from Wimbledon. In between the cricket, I could manage to squeeze in a few visits to the most hallowed turf in tennis.

Like Lord's, authority at Wimbledon could be stiff upper-lipped, but unlike at cricket's most venerated venue, less stodgy. The stewards at Wimbledon I found more willing to assist in getting a 'feel' of the place, but also discuss issues and people. One of those I met still recalled Vijay Amritraj fondly.

'He was a big fellow, a fine player and a gentleman,' he said. 'Is that why he didn't win any of the Grand Slams?' I asked the steward, referring to Amritraj's friendly demeanour. 'Well if he wasn't as pleasantly mannered, Vijay would have been American, not Indian,' he replied. Was that a compliment or complaint, I am left wondering even now.

The English summer is, of course, replete with sporting action and the cricket World Cup was the high-point of the season. In the Asian community at least—and understandably so—this could have been the only thing that mattered. But seen holistically, the country was going through a churn that was to have significant repercussions in the coming years.

For instance, Thatcherism was taking firm control of political and economic life in England in the early 1980s, and Prime Minister and 'Iron Lady' Margaret Thatcher was the undisputed Queen Bee. Only occasionally was she forced to share centre stage with US President Ronald Reagan.

In that sense, even the World Cup enjoyed miniscule importance, but for those weaned on cricket lore, England was still a dream come true. The grounds of Sussex spoke of the exploits of Ranjitsinhji and the two Pataudis apart, of course, from CB Fry. At Lord's, passing through the Grace Gates was like a pilgrimage in itself, though the good doctor himself was actually from Gloucestershire.

But my personal favourite as a diehard Surrey fan was the Oval, home to Jack Hobbs, the Bedsers and my childhood hero, Ken Barrington. I had spent years reading the *Wisden Almanack* and *Playfair Cricket Annual*—bought from Mumbai's (formerly Bombay) second-hand booksellers many months after being released in England—and had rejoiced in Surrey's successes or found villains in other teams when they didn't. The World Cup carousel took me to most of the historic grounds one had only read or heard about. When no matches were scheduled, I made day-trips to soak in the history and nostalgia.

There were only six journalists (if I remember correctly) from India. The explosion in the Indian media, with its din, clamour and suffocating competition to grab sound bites, was nearly two decades away. In 1983 there was still easy access to players and the dressing room. Some tenuous kind of camaraderie between players and the press existed then, especially when the team was touring overseas.

Hefty match fees and allowances, single rooms in five-star hotels et al are a relatively new development in Indian cricket. Indeed, historians might trace the origins of this to the 1983 World Cup victory. But while the tournament was being played, such luxuries were still unthinkable and kept the players less insulated from the world, and especially the media.

In fact, I was once part of a group of media-persons, Indian cricket supporters from England and a couple of players who spent a night on the tiles in Central London. The revelry continued into the wee hours of the morning. And please don't ask me for names. That would be a dishonourable thing to do even thirty years later! But there was no match commitment for a few days so there was no breach of curfew or protocol, though I am sure manager PR Man Singh, a stickler for discipline, would not have approved.

I also remember watching Dilip Vengsarkar get hit on the face by Malcolm Marshall from the dressing room. There was a flurry of abuse when the batsman returned retired hurt, and not from Vengsarkar, poor chap, who could barely open his mouth. When India played Zimbabwe in the historic match at Tunbridge Wells, I watched a fair bit of Kapil Dev's memorable innings sitting next to Gundappa Viswanath—fondly called Vishy—from just outside the dressing room.

Vishy, who hadn't yet retired, had failed to regain his place after the disastrous tour of Pakistan, but was still an integral member of the Indian team. He was also the main source of hope, I realised, as the team tottered. When India was 9 for 4, he was to say with a sense of righteous belief, 'Don't worry, the match is not over yet'. He must have been the only person then to believe this. Talk of prophetic words.

Kapil Dev's unbeaten 175 in that match, of course, was not just a tour de force, but a tournament-changer, as it were. Official broadcaster BBC was on strike so there is no video evidence, alas, of this innings, robbing posterity of one of cricket's most dramatic stories.

As the tournament progressed, the small media corps became almost like an extended family of the team, but this did not mean we did not look for 'controversies'. The composition of the team showed a distinct north-west divide, so to speak, and anybody who knows anything of Indian cricket knows how much these things mattered in those days. Did it influence Kapil Dev? More importantly, was Sunil Gavaskar dropped for the first match against Australia, or 'rested', as the manager insisted?

All such doubts died by the time Kapil Dev had finished his business at Tunbridge Wells. Gavaskar was back in the team, despite his mediocre form; Vengsarkar was still out of contention through injury; but by a process of trial and exigency, India had hit on the right combination.

The academically inclined are still locked in endless debate about which has been the greatest ever one-day innings. In my mind there is no doubt that Kapil Dev's unbeaten 175 that day stands supreme. There have been bigger scores since, innings with more sixes and boundaries hit, runs scored at a faster rate, but for sheer magnitude of impact (in myriad ways) nothing quite matches up to Kapil's innings.

It not only helped India win victory from the jaws of defeat, but also dramatically altered the course of the tournament, and subsequently, the future of Indian and world cricket. This innings was to be a rallying cry from a field-marshal to his troops, as it were. Remember, Kapil was in his first season as captain, having taken over from Gavaskar after the rout against Pakistan a few months earlier.

This change in captaincy had been contentious, and for many critics manifested the north-west divide. The 'rivalry' between Gavaskar and Kapil was to become one of the long-running soap operas in Indian cricket in the 1980s. I am unsure just how intense this rift between India's two leading cricketers of the time was; in later years, both players were to deny it. But it certainly didn't help that administrators and selectors were also seen to be partisan, one way or the other.

Moreover, India had come into the World Cup on the back of a series defeat against the West Indies, and there were muted discussions on Kapil's future as leader even before the tournament began. The pressure on him was to not only justify his reputation as one of the game's greatest all-rounders, but also to hold his team together and thereby hold on to his captaincy.

Examine the scorebook and you find that India's performances till then had been modest—despite the first-match win over the West Indies—and not at all indicative of the heady climax that was to follow. There had been a couple of exciting fifties, some of the swing bowlers like Roger Binny and Madan Lal were enjoying the helpful conditions and the fielding was much improved by traditional Indian standards. But there was nothing to suggest this was a world-beating side.

The next week flew past in a flurry of wins, banter, laughter and disbelief as India knocked over a struggling Australia and an overconfident England to earn a place in the final against the world champions. This was surreal stuff from a side which had now forged such enormous self-belief as to become unstoppable.

Australia was a team in disarray, with Greg Chappell not available and unconfirmed reports suggesting massive infighting between some of the senior pros and skipper Kim Hughes. Having lost their first game against Zimbabwe, the Aussies were on the backfoot when they met India at Chelmsford. As it happened, neither Dennis Lillee nor Hughes played that game and the result was a massive defeat which was to culminate in Hughes surrendering the captaincy in tears a year later.

The two semi-finals involved India and Pakistan. Could it be a dream final between the two arch-rivals from the subcontinent? It was not to be, as Pakistan lost badly to the West Indies. With Imran Khan unable to bowl, Pakistan relied heavily on their batting, but in this crucial match missed Javed Miandad, who reported unwell. I happened to meet Miandad in his hotel room on the eve of the match. He was obviously suffering from influenza. I wondered, though, if he could miss such an important game; he did and that was that.

On the same day, India's players marched to Old Trafford like born-again gladiators, bristling for the kill. It was a surcharged atmosphere and by the time the match ended in a flurry of boundaries by Sandeep Patil off the hapless Bob Willis, many fights had broken out between the fans of the two sides all over the ground. One placard captured the Indian performance and the result of the match tellingly: 'Kapil Dev eats Ian Botham for breakfast'.

After the semi-final ended, I had an encounter of a different kind at Manchester. There were no day-night matches then, and since the bus to take me back to London wasn't to leave till past 10 p.m. I ventured into a bar near the station to while away time. Not till I was propositioned a few times did it dawn on me that I had strayed into a gay bar, which became a matter of great mirth with fellow journalists and players.

The couple of days between the semi-final and the final passed in a blur. The Indian community in England was obviously overjoyed and Kapil's Devils, as the team had come to be tagged after beating England, were obviously in high demand. At one of these parties,

I recall Kapil Dev being asked by a guest how he intended to beat West Indies in the final.

'It's the other way around,' said the Indian captain. 'Now they have to beat us.' He was obviously being hyperbolic but, in some ways, Kapil's seemingly off-the-cuff statement also reflected the mindset of the Indian players: not only had self-belief grown enormously, there was also a sense of unbridled derring-do that could be so crucial in what was otherwise seen as a lop-sided contest.

On the morning of the final, after the previous night's indulgences, I woke up with a start to find Surbiton, where I was staying, was a good hour and more away from Lord's by train, involving a switch from British rail to the Underground. Hurrying through shower and breakfast, I decided to take a taxi to save time, little realising that driving through London would take longer than by train.

By the time I jumped out of the cab at Grace Gates, I was out of breath, time—and money. The journey set me back 40 quid, which was far more than a day's allowance for me in those days. More pertinently, the toss had already taken place, as the steward informed me, half in admonishment, and play was about to begin.

I raced to the winding staircase that led up the press box which was situated in the stand near long leg, close to the pavilion and yet some distance from the main gate (The location of this box has since been shifted to bang opposite the pavilion and, by common consensus, the media enclosure now resembles Cherie Blair's lips).

Running up the stairs, I bumped into the venerated Richie Benaud, who was commentating for the BBC. '60-1 on India if that excites you', or some such he said, as I stood panting to greet him briefly. It is a truism that life offers rare moments to make a killing. I was too nonplussed to take Benaud's offer, or perhaps too chicken. Really, what chance did the Indian team stand against the mighty West Indies?

The opportunity to make some big money had come and passed in a flash, as it were. The toss had been won by West Indies and India, batting first, could muster only a paltry 183. There were laments and cluck-clucks during the break that this was turning out to be a no-contest. The 'I told you so' were boasting that they had told us so: India stood no chance.

But there was to be a tantalising twist to the story as the brash West Indies came to grief against an inspired Indian side. As the wickets kept tumbling—first Greenidge, then Richards, then Haynes, Lloyd and Gomes—Indian hearts, both on the field and off it, swelled with hope.

Within a seven-hour roller-coaster ride, the cricket world was turned upside down; India won the World Cup, a billion lives changed forever. On a personal level, the second issue which had dogged my flight into England was resolved too: the law degree would find its place on the mantelpiece; writing on cricket was to be my calling.

Postscript

In the wake of the '83 triumph, India's administrators were emboldened to confront the English administrators and get the World Cup shifted to the subcontinent. Lore has it that the then BCCI president NKP Salve was so miffed at being refused passes for the final against West Indies that he swore to break England's hegemony.

His cohorts in pursuing this ambition were senior BCCI functionaries Jagmohan Dalmiya and IS Bindra, then also thick friends. In 1987 India and Pakistan jointly hosted the World Cup, but this would not have been possible without the tacit support of Pakistan Cricket Board chief Air Marshall (Retired) Nur Khan.

The late Rajiv Gandhi, in a major move to show his rising clout as a power centre, promised to clear the foreign exchange needed for the Cup. To fit the tournament into the subcontinent's winter, where light fades early (remember, there were no facilities to play at night then), matches were reduced to fifty overs a side.

The 1983 World Cup triggered off a boom which saw India become the epicentre for world cricket. Fuelled by economic growth arising out of economic liberalisation, the country was also to become its El Dorado over the next twenty years, providing 75 per cent of the global viewership and 70 per cent of the revenue.

It took twenty-eight years for India to win the World Cup again. India's triumph in 2011 was spectacular, but for its sheer impact on the Indian psyche and the game, the 1983 victory remains unsurpassed.

Ayaz Memon has been a journalist for more than thirty-three years. A lawyer by qualification, he got seduced by sports into pursuing a different vocation and has since gone on to be sports editor of some of India's leading publications like *The Times of India* as well as editor of *Mid-Day* and *DNA*. He has authored three books on cricket and co-authored one on fifty years of India's independence titled *India 50: The Making of a Nation.*

Man of Bronze

Rohit Brijnath

> The medal did not weigh on his mind at first. When Leander arrived in Atlanta, he adhered to convention by partying religiously; then he beat Pereira and it struck him: 'Yes, a medal is possible.' But he told no one.

Here in Rio Bravo, a Mexican restaurant in Atlanta, on an August evening in 1996, where cigarette smoke hangs like an opaque curtain and the burgeoning noise perforates eardrums, the night is becoming a blur for Leander Adrian Paes. Finally, the last dregs of adrenalin that have coursed through his veins all fortnight are drying up. A small, circular bronze medallion rests on the seat of a car outside: it is nothing much to look at, it is everything there is in his life.

Word has wafted through the restaurant about him and strangers arrive with napkins and pens and waiters arrive with Key Lime Pie, a Southern dessert, on the house. His hands, lightning in the morning, are like slow-rolling thunder now. Still he signs. Earlier in the evening, at an Indian reception, people surround him. Touching the medal. Touching him. It is easy to explain: it is impatient devotion, it is forty-four years of a nation waiting for an Olympic medal. Any colour will do.

Way back in 1952, when Jawaharlal Nehru was prime minister, KD Jadhav had won a wrestling bronze. Now India, ten prime ministers later, was still waiting for it to happen again. How heavy a burden is that? Heavy enough to force a twenty-three-year-old from Calcutta, who ends matches with a sign of the cross, into offering gentle lies. Asked about the enormity of his bronze medal match a day earlier at a press conference, he replied poker-faced: 'It is just another match.' How in hell's name could he speak of the butterflies playing hopscotch in his stomach, of the arrows of uncertainty that pierced his mind? On the morning of the match, as he sat in the locker room, nervousness stood sharply etched in his face.

'Hey, relax,' a friend said, 'just go out and do your best.'

'No,' he whispered, 'I have to win, I'm too close.'

In the Davis Cup, which he has been playing since 1990, pressure is only the journalist's cliche for him, it is not a threat. The pressure doesn't grind him down, he once said dramatically, and he is inherently and always dramatic, especially when he plays, and you can see it in his eyes, his contorted facial muscles, his almost musical body language. The pressure, he explains, is like arms lifting him up, but now, in interviews, in conversations, now at the Olympics, he hears only this: forty-four years. He has spent the previous evening with doubles partner Mahesh Bhupathi and they're friends tied together by some umbilical cord and they know better, but still the talk is about forty-four years.

In the morning, the team physician tells him: 'You're the one who can do it, please get us the medal.'

Sweet Jesus.

There's an Indian flag at the tennis centre at Stone Mountain Park, US. There's an India affixed to his name, for here, like the Davis Cup, he doesn't represent just himself. And through the years he'll tell you about this Indian flag and goosebumps and it sounds familiar and trite. Except Indian athletes have always been programmed to strike a nationalistic chord, to be a populist hero, and when struggling to articulate themselves they reach for this safe response. But even so, when Leander did play for India, a switch did flick, some circuits in his brain, normally dormant, began to crackle furiously.

This was partly because he has never truly been a player. He is in fact a performer, he is an actor, and the Davis Cup is his preferred theatre. On the tour, in some qualifying match on a distant court, he returns to averageness. But offer him a crowd, a cause and he transcends his averageness. Which is why he, ranked so far down the ladder that it takes some searching, will up-end Wayne Ferreira, the Queen's champion, on grass in straight sets in Davis Cup 6-3, 6-4, 7-5; will confuse Arnaud Boetsch on French clay 6-4, 7-5, 6-4; will come back from two sets down to beat Goran Ivanisevic 6-7, 4-6, 7-6, 6-4, 6-1 on grass. He'll write for himself a small, bewildering, magical history in this competition.

But this, the Olympics, is different, isn't it? It's playing for India, yes, but this isn't just two singles matches and a doubles like the Davis Cup, it is a string of matches, and of all the enemies he has collected over time, with his maddening technique, in instinctively absurd shot selection (his penchant for drop shots will bemuse Andre Agassi in Atlanta), in the absence of any baseline rhythm, his worst foe is inconsistency. He is brilliant in patches, he can compose dazzling lines of tennis but only that. He can write haiku with a tennis racket now and then, but never *The Rime of the Ancient Mariner*.

So, no, this medal, he couldn't win, not from the No 126 in the world.

It is why I don't even go to the tennis in Atlanta. Hockey calls, Carl Lewis commands, runner Michael Johnson beckons, weightlifter Naim Süleymanoğlu teases, but wherever I wander over to this slightly antiseptic games, in every arena, news leaks in about Leander. He wins a match. Uhh, nice. Then, he wins again. Well done, kid. Then he wins again, and you think, this is ridiculous. Every opponent is ranked higher and this, really, is his gift, to be an Indian aberration of sorts in the 1990s. Because he can play above himself, he shrugs off the intimidation which has held our athletes tightly like a forearm around the throat, he sees no value in the inferiority complex. Because he has this ability occasionally to free himself and then temporarily find himself. And in his liberation we find ours.

I make the trek to the tennis also because it is personal. Calcutta is a small town in the guise of a big city, it is where he comes from, it is where I belong. Football is the resident religion here and the brave sit in precarious stands, which give the illusion of swaying with every cheer as Mohun Bagan eyeball East Bengal, a mad concerto whose finale often is a charge from spitting mounted police on neighing horses with ancient light sabers called lathis.

But it is also an elegant tennis town, a town of more refined pleasures, a South Club town, where old-timers with tent-pole legs sticking out of starched tennis shorts swear the grass some years is sweeter than Wimbledon's. On these courts my father, who served with one leg affixed to the ground as was the quaint fashion and imprisoned his wooden racket in a press which resembled a medieval instrument of torture, took me to watch Davis Cup. On these courts, later, I am introduced to Naresh Kumar, Jaideep Mukherjea, Premjit Lall, Akhtar Ali, each grand man full of tales and spins.

It is to this Calcutta world Leander was added. This boy who slept with his football boots under his pillow; this boy who suffered from Osgood-Schlatter disease which necessitated a steel brace along his leg which he dragged ferociously across court like some limping tennis conscript. At a Calcutta club, he was once kicked off the courts and with youthful impertinence told older men, one day when I win Wimbledon you'll invite me back. He makes half-good on that promise in 1990 by winning the Wimbledon junior title.

I see him win there in SW19 and in the Davis Cup; I see him enraged when we lose to his sisters in carrom because competitiveness with such men is like a persistent infection; I see him and his father Dr Vece Paes and his stepmother Julie struggle to make a career for this Calcutta hopeful. So now I have to see him again. Except he gets on court against the Brazilian, Fernando Meligeni, in the bronze medal play-off and begins the biggest match of his life, playing the worst tennis of the fortnight.

What is happening here, he must think?

The player who arrived at the Olympics was a slightly unfamiliar Leander. A diamond stud in his ear (a pact he and Bhupathi made when they earned an Olympics double slot) and some muscle in his biceps. Tennis is a game of plateaus: you ascend, plateau, ascend, plateau, each level so much harder than the next. For three years Leander was stationary; now suddenly he was on the move. Mike Rada, a fitness trainer, had joined him, and, says Leander: 'He got me off my butt into the gym, doing weights and making me stronger.'

His serve which once travelled at the speed of a jogging geriatric—that's when it came in—was now a revelation; through six matches he averaged 61.5 per cent of first serves, his second serve 93 per cent and he hit one at 199 kmph, making him the ninth fastest server at the tournament. Put it down to that bicep and a new toss.

His forehand, hit always more with prayer and audacity, had found a temporary groove. And he, who played with the undue haste of a man late for dinner with Pamela Anderson, had been visited somewhat by patience: if once he ran intemperately straight for the net, now he varied his game, pausing to rally, visiting the net only when it was time. Anderson would have to wait, for Leander was dining on the opposition: outplaying Richey Reneberg (No 20), Nicolas Pereira (No 74), Thomas Enquist (No 10), Renzo Furlan (No 26), losing a single set in four matches.

And then arrived his Lordship Agassi, World No 6.

The medal did not weigh on his mind at first. When Leander arrived in Atlanta, he adhered to convention by partying religiously; then he beat Pereira and it struck him: 'Yes, a medal is possible.' But he told no one. 'I didn't want to raise expectations.' By the time he finished with Agassi, losing barely 6-7, 3-6, the secret was out, for he played with a desire so awfully naked. Indians are quiet, undemonstrative; Leander plays like a man soaked in kerosene who fires himself up by lighting matchsticks with his teeth. In the guest lounge later, an odd pandemonium reigned.

Fathers Mike Agassi and Dr Vece Paes would meet, the former telling the latter: 'Amazing. My boy is supposed to play well, but your boy has been playing this week like a Top 4 player.' Tennis legend Billie Jean King would look at coach Jaideep Mukherjea and say, 'You've got a raw talent there. He is a Top 30 player for sure.' And former Wimbledon champion Virginia Wade would ruffle Leander's hair, saying: 'You were lovely.' Leander, who played David with the slingshot to Agassi's Goliath almost to Biblical perfection, smiled; inside he was weeping.

'If I had lost 6-2, 6-2 to Agassi, it would have been fine, but to have come so close...' He stops. He is thinking of the two set points he missed in the first set. 'My strength is putting away matches at crucial times and I didn't.' In any other tennis tournament, he would be out; now, oddly, despite losing, he is still in for he has a bronze medal play-off remaining. He must find a way to bury disappointment and refocus anew; he must wonder about his strained tendon in his right wrist, injured by a stinging Agassi backhand drive. He must wonder about forty-four years.

The first set against Fernando Meligeni has gone 3-6, the bronze medal disappearing, his game flat. A day started badly is continuing so. 'I got up edgy in the morning. Normally I go through my routine, but I couldn't keep from thinking about the match.' When rain delayed the match, his condition worsened: 'I didn't work on strategy, I just wanted the match over by now.' It showed: he stayed back instead of going forward; his wrists, usually supple, now appeared heavy with cement. 'I wasn't thinking, I was playing emotional tennis.'

We understand this emotion. In the press box, there is to be no cheering, it is unprofessional. We're writers, we're observers, not fans, not always immune to the result but through practice adept in controlling reaction. But this day, as he wins the second set 6-2, is just different. It is forty-four years of collected mediocrity with the occasional sunshine moment which makes it personal; it is forty-four years of rolling in paper into the typewriter and hammering out frustrating epitaphs till your fingers are just familiar painters of negativity which make it personal; it is also Leander who makes tennis personal, offering up the absurd idea that he is playing for you.

So some of us exit the press box, we sit in the stands. No, that's not enough. In the third set, I exit the stands, mouth sucking cigarette, ear tuned to the scores on the loudspeaker, almost too scared to watch. But he isn't scared. He wins the third set 6-4 and the match. I cry. What else?

Meligeni, gracious, describes it best: 'You never know what he is doing the next point. It is not easy to play him.' But more, on a day in which technically he played the worst tennis of the tournament, Leander, like he has so often done when playing for India, won the match from his stomach. Later, in the locker room, his tears arriving without warning, I ask, 'How did you win today?'

'Guts,' he says.

Later he stands on the podium beside Agassi (three Grand Slam titles then) and Sergi Bruguera (two Grand Slam titles) and it is an incongruous yet lifting moment, for Leander is yet to win a round at a Grand Slam tournament. He, though, is thinking of Agassi. Of a chance gone.

Ceremony done, he will scoot to an outside court on my request to let photographer Tommy Hindley rapidly shoot frames of the medal that sits on his chest. We hurry, dinner is waiting at the Rio Bravo, his father is waiting; a father who won a medal of a similar colour with the Indian hockey team in 1972. That medal rumouredly is gone, misplaced in the chaos of a Calcutta flood. Doesn't matter. What the father lost, the son replaces.

(This article is an extended version of a piece which first appeared in India Today *magazine in August 1996.)*

Postscript

Leander Paes, born in June, 1973, has competed in six Olympic Games—1992, 1996, 2000, 2004, 2008, 2012. Post his Olympic medal in 1996, he went on to win his only singles title in Newport on grass in 1998 and reached his highest singles ranking of No 73. Morphing into a doubles specialist, Paes became World No. 1 in 1999 and has won fifty titles including seven Grand Slam titles with four different partners: Wimbledon 1999 (Mahesh Bhupathi), French Open 1999 (Bhupathi), French Open 2001 (Bhupathi), US Open 2006 (Martin Damm), French Open 2009 (Lukas Dlouhy), US Open 2009 (Dlouhy), Australian Open 2012 (Radek Stepanek). He also owns six Grand Slam mixed double titles. Eventually, Paes did not become the singles player of merit he was widely expected to be, but stayed relevant in Indian tennis through his Davis Cup performances and doubles exploits. His triumphs at times were interrupted by an abrasive relationship with former friend and doubles partner

Mahesh Bhupathi. Their break-ups and make-ups had an element of farce to them, but Paes' contribution to tennis will outlive it all. In this writer's reckoning he is probably the fourth-greatest tennis player India has produced, tailing, in order, Ramanathan Krishnan, Vijay Amritraj and Ramesh Krishnan.

Rohit Brijnath was fortunate to cover his first Wimbledon in 1987 when he was twenty-four years old. He joined *India Today* in 1993 and continued writing on a variety of sports. He left for Melbourne in 2000 where he contributed articles to *The Hindu*, BCC South Asia Website, *The Mint* and *The Age*. Since 2008 he has been a senior correspondent at *The Straits Times* in Singapore. In late 2011, he finished his first book, co-writing *A Shot at History* with Olympic gold medallist Abhinav Bindra.

The Mystery of the Barefoot Footballers

Arindam Basu

> 'We played attacking football at that time. That was the style of play. We knew if we let in a goal we could score two. We were ready to take on the world.'

Legend has it that they swept the ground like an approaching tornado. On the turf they played like giants, the opposition completely dwarfed. The fans, dazzled by their talent and charm, came back for more. They were the legends of Indian football, often referred to as immortals by later generations. I first saw Sailen Manna, one of the immortals, as a kid during a prize distribution ceremony in our locality. I had always heard snatches of a story that the Indian football team was denied a chance of playing in the 1950 World Cup because they could not buy boots. I looked at the frail figure of Sailen Manna and envisioned in my mind his youthful, despondent image. Years passed by and it was a forgotten chapter, until I stumbled upon a report in an old newspaper while doing some research work on football.

It was a Press Trust of India (PTI) report published in a Bengali newspaper that got me ticking. The initial search resulted in some deadpan facts. The World Cup of football had not been staged since 1938. The 1942 and 1946 editions were both cancelled due to World War II. After the war, FIFA was keen to resurrect the competition as soon as possible and they began making plans for a World Cup tournament to take place. For some time, the World Cup was at risk of not being held out of sheer disinterest from the international community, until Brazil presented a bid at the 1946 FIFA Congress, offering to host the event on condition that the tournament take place in 1950.

India was in Group 10 of the qualification round for the 1950 World Cup. But three other teams in the group—Burma, Indonesia and Philippines—withdrew, giving India an automatic berth into the final. But, quite inexplicably, India did not participate in the World Cup. For a young nation to let go of such an opportunity would have come at considerable cost.

Stories did their rounds and slowly moulded into an impregnable myth of barefoot footballers who were not allowed to play in the World Cup by FIFA; boots were a must. Some said the sea journey was too much to be undertaken. Others sympathised with a poor AIFF (All India Football Federation), Indian football's governing body, which could not raise the funds.

An article in *Daily Pioneer* stated: 'It may be recalled in 1950 that the Indian football team qualified for the World Cup in Brazil. But the country did not have enough foreign exchange to send the team there. And thereafter India never qualified again.'

Further digging on the Net yielded a BBC report that said: 'India pulled out because FIFA would not let them play bare feet.' In another article attributed to the BBC: 'The country qualified regularly for the Olympics until the 1960s, and were invited to the 1950 World Cup in Brazil but the problems of a long sea journey and the fact that they still played bare feet prevented them from appearing.'

It was a bottle of ether and I was left to fathom for myself what had happened behind the closed doors of Indian football that the team never set sail for Brazil. Though the barefoot theory sounded the most convincing, it was never concluded with evidence that playing barefoot was a deterrent. Then there was yet another piece of news I stumbled upon.

A PTI report datelined Calcutta, 23 May 1950 said AIFF cited differentiation in team selection and lack of time for practice as reasons for withdrawal. In fact, the AIFF blamed Brazil for the debacle. The release read, 'India will not participate in the World Cup or the Jules Rimet Cup. Due to late information reaching India, the team will have to be flown to Rio resulting in cancellation of team selection. Since there is not much time, the Indian team will not be able to prepare and hence it will not be correct to send the team.'

PTI added: 'Moin-ul-Haq [then AIFF president] after a closed door meeting with Bombay and Calcutta football federations has decided not to send the team. It may be mentioned here that IFA (Indian Football Association) was given responsibility to select the Indian team. It was decided that an amount of ₹50,000 would be collected from four charity matches as funds for the forthcoming World Cup.'

I decided to dig into the story further, wanting to reach the bottom of it. During the hours spent rummaging through piles of old newspapers in libraries, there was this report published on 11 May 1950 in the then largest circulated Bengali daily *Jugantar*. It stated: 'India will participate in the 1950 World Cup or Jules Rimet Cup. The organisers are planning to take the Indian football team to Brazil from Calcutta. Due to this decision, the AIFF will save around ₹40,000. India will play its first game on June 28. For the benefit of the Indian team Bombay Football Association (BFA) will bear ₹5,000. Besides, money will be raised through charity matches to be played in Calcutta as per request of the Indian Football Association. The money will be used for the Indian team's journey. On May 16 the IFA World Cup Committee will select the players for the team.'

If India had decided not to participate in the World Cup as they were barefooted, then a team selection would not have been done. In fact, in a memoir by Sailen Manna, the footballer recalled that a camp began under the coaching of famous English coach Harry Wright and went on for three days before being suddenly disbanded.

According to a report in *Jugantar* of 16 May, the Madras Football Association made a request to AIFF to consider the following players for selection: Manuswamy and Gopalnathan (MSM RAIL), Vajravelu, Mani, Alaviriswami and Angraj (TVS Madura), Anjenelu (Wimco), Murugesan (B&C Mills), Gafur and Gulam (Sporting Youngster) and Hanumant Rao (Tilak Moti).

AIFF president Moin-ul-Haq reached Calcutta on 23 May, a day after India was tagged in Group C along with Italy, Sweden and Paraguay. Brazil's then foreign minister presided over a meeting that was held in the library room of the foreign office in Rio de Janerio. The lots were drawn and India was in Group C with the superpowers of Europe and Latin America.

This was a golden opportunity. In the 1948 London Olympics the team had given a reasonable account of themselves and the World Cup would have established India on the map of professional football. A long closed door meeting took place with IFA and BFA representatives along with Moin-ul-Haq. And then suddenly a press release was sent that India would not participate in the World Cup.

Kaushik Bandyopadhyay, associate academic editor, *Soccer and Society* (Routledge) and fellow, Olympic Solidarity, International Olympic Committee, Lausanne, says, 'Most commonly ascribed reasons for this withdrawal are lack of foreign reserves, barefooted playing style, the long sea journey and apprehension about India's chances against the world's topmost teams. However, a careful study of contemporary newspaper reports reveals that beneath the apparent financial difficulties, cited by the AIFF as the main reason for withdrawing from the World Cup, lay an unusual failure of the AIFF to appreciate the importance of India's participation in the Cup, despite assurance from the organising committee to bear a major part of the tour expenses. A sea journey was out of the question as Brazil offered to fly the Indian team to Rio.'

The late Sailen Manna was supposed to be the captain of that team. At eighty-six, his memory failed him. But he still remembered the fact that they did not go to play in the World Cup. 'We had no idea about the World Cup then. If we had we would have taken the initiative ourselves. For us the Olympics were everything. It was dubbed the greatest show on earth. There was nothing bigger than the Olympics. We had done well in London and were happy,' Manna forced his memory back through the unending field of furrows on his forehead.

'We lost a golden opportunity and certainly not because we played barefoot. We had a team that was worth a try. We had six world class strikers in Ahmed, Salle, Sattar, Mewalal and Runu Guhathakurta. In defence, I was aided by Papen and Aziz. Varadaraj was a tower of strength before the goal. The midfield had Latif, Shanmugam, Noor and Chandan Singh,' he added with deep remorse.

'We played attacking football at that time. That was the style of play. We knew if we let in a goal we could score two. We were ready to take on the world. I believe they must have feared that if the team went to play the World Cup they would be termed professionals and Olympics was played only by amateurs,' Manna, who has been named India's Player of the Century, had said in an interview.

Another report from 1950 tried to give a more balanced approach, says Kaushik. 'India's last minute decision to stay out of World Cup in Brazil has much to commend but more to condemn it. Commend because India ultimately found herself in a position by which our footballers would have to make a mad rush from one end of the world to the other with little or no organised preparation. Condemn because taking the entire picture of the last fourteen months, India, but for some masterly inactivity on part of the AIFF, should have never found herself in such a jam, which did no good to either Indian football or her sports prestige abroad.'

Barefoot was certainly not the reason for walking out of the World Cup. In the 1911 Mohun Bagan team there was only one player wearing boots, Rev Sudhir Chatterjee. The Mohammedan Sporting team in the 1930s also wore boots. Moreover, players from other states, too, used to wear boots.

Just for the record, on 24 June 1950—the day the World Cup kicked off in Brazil—the Bombay Football Association banned playing barefoot football under their aegis, while in Calcutta, East Bengal scored a facile 2:0 victory over Dalhousie Club. Both the goals were scored by Mohanraj, who wore boots.

With very little documentation available from those days it is indeed difficult to reconstruct the course of events. India had gained freedom in 1947. In 1950 it established itself as a republic. In May the same year the French gave up their territory of Chandannagar, some 70 kilometres from Calcutta, thus bringing it under the Indian Union. Refugee problems, riots and building a nation were the priorities.

Hence there is no record of the team made to assemble in Calcutta for selection. We are left with two line-ups, one from the London Olympics and the other of the Asian Games in 1951, to imagine the possible players who might have made it to the 1950 World Cup.

The Indian team gave a great account of themselves in the Olympics in 1948 and barely lost to France, but not without dazzling Europe with their skills. The team consisted of: B Anthony, Papan, S Manna, A Latif, Chandan Singh, Noor Mohammed, P Venkatesh, Runu Guhathakurta, S Mewalal, Ahmed Khan, S Nandy (Coach: BD Chatterjee).

In 1951, India won the gold in the Asian Games defeating Iran by a Mewalal goal. The team consisted of: Anthony and KL Varadaraj (goal); S Manna, Sunil Chatterjee, SK Azizuddin, TM Verghese (defence); Latif, Chandan Singh, A Ghosh, DN Jones, T Shammugham, Noor Mohammed (midfield); Venkatesh, MA Sattar, PBA Saleh, Runu Guhathakurta, Mewalal, Nandy, Ahmed Khan, GYS Laiq, Loganathan, AM Bachan (forward) (Coach: SA Rahim).

But there is no line-up of probables for the World Cup. Those amateur days were glorious days. India was a nervous entrant in the 2011 Asian Cup, a meet where they were runners-up in 1964. It also triumphed at the 1951 and 1962 Asiads and surged to the Olympics football semi-finals in Melbourne, in 1956. In Melbourne, Willy Meisl, the theorist and author of *Soccer Revolution*, told coach SA Rahim after India's win over Australia that it was the best display by an Asian team he had seen. Six years earlier India might have earned similar compliments at the World Cup in Brazil. Simple inertia from the authorities saw the chance go abegging.

Such opportunities will not come again. That is the problem with opportunities. In a world where sport grows at a rapid pace and nations arm themselves with professionalism, India languishes.

Once among Asia's best in the 1950s, India is at the bottom of the heap at the 165th place of the FIFA rankings.

What has been repeatedly heard was a clever orchestration made by the AIFF as a cover up for their ineptness. While the inability to play with boots was shown as the chief reason, what slowly went under the carpet was that, first, a team needed to be selected for the World Cup and then a decision on whether they would play barefeet or not.

Kaushik adds, 'A lot has also been made of the infighting between the Bombay Football Association and IFA. But I don't think so. The BFA later wanted to give ₹10,000 for the footballers to be ferried to Brazil. It was a great opportunity lost for Indian football. There were many who considered India's participation to be a must for the realisation of its immense future potential.'

Ajoy Bose in one of his columns titled 'The Jules Rimet Cup', written in the same year, had said: 'It is obvious that India is not up to the best professional standards but even losing heavily would have been a great education to these players. Where education and experience are the only things to be gained without any hope of winning, it was the ideal condition. But it was largely because of the foolishness of the Indian Football Federation that India did not take part in the World Cup in Brazil.'

As a parting note, let me leave a small pointer to India's zero-interest in the World Cup. After 1950, India started playing World Cup qualifiers only from 1986. In between India gave the World Cup a giant cold shoulder, resulting in a huge setback. The World Cup berth continues to remain a fable for Indian football. Just to set the record straight, their inexplicable absence may not have surfaced only because of barefooted footballers, but for some foolish administrators who failed to gauge the importance of the opportunity.

Postscript

Today Indian football stands at the throes of a new era. Under the newly appointed technical director Robert Baan, a new football policy has been drafted that will, hopefully, be in place soon. This will give Indian football the much needed spine to stand up, with four regional academies and an elite academy to scout, train and develop talent. Moreover, a concerted effort is also in place to make sure that the clubs develop their youth teams and take part in the national process of building a strong football-playing nation. With India emerging as the potential market, global football giants and teams like Manchester United and Real Madrid are looking at India now. Time seems to have arrived to take football to the next level. If AIFF fails this time, India's tryst with World Cup will forever remain a chalice of desire.

Currently Special Correspondent (Sports) with *The Bengal Post*, **Arindam Basu** has been in sports journalism for the last decade and a half covering various disciplines. But football has always been his first love.

The Man We Forgot

Clayton Murzello

> I cried everyday…everyday. I used to bawl like a cow. I believe God used my tears to wash away my sorrows. Can I test that scientifically? No, but I believe that.

I had an urge to interview Winston Davis as soon as I overheard English journalist Matthew Engel talking to Indian batting legend Sunil Gavaskar about participating in a benefit game to raise funds for Davis during the 1998 Mini World Cup in Bangladesh. A little over a year ago, Davis suffered a cruel blow…literally…when a branch of a tree he was chopping hit him in the back of his head and left him paralysed.

Davis was familiar with Indian players. Eleven of his fifteen Tests he played from 1982-83 to 1987-88 were against India. That apart, his finest hour—7 for 51 against Australia—was in the 1983 World Cup which India won. Despite that performance, he was not in the playing XI in the final, which India famously won on 25 June 1983, at Lord's.

Although Davis was a junior in Clive Lloyd's pace pack, he played all the six Tests of the 1983-84 series in India, unlike senior pros Andy Roberts and Wayne Daniel. He claimed fourteen wickets at 40.14.

The *Oxford Dictionary of Cricketers* describes him as 'Lean, lithe, and of a relatively short run with a quick arm action, liable to bowl the occasional ball of lethal whiplash speed. Winston Davis, a St Vincentian, would have been a regular Test bowler for most countries in most eras but his appearances in the early 1980s were limited by the extraordinary depth of fast bowling talent in the Caribbean.'

The opportunity to trace Davis presented itself when I was in Northampton where India played a tour game against the county in August 2011.

On a chilly, rainy day, I headed to the indoor nets where the Indians trained. A tall West Indian, Wendell Pemberton, was too much of a character to ignore. Wendell spoke about how he bowled to VVS Laxman when the Hyderabadi stylist figured in a charity match at Northampton in 2005. He also reminded me that Davis, along with Curtly Ambrose, played for his county.

I expressed my desire to meet Davis and Wendell was glad to help. But he gave me enough indication that accessing the former West Indies pacer would not be easy. Wendell's willingness to help bordered on journalistic foolishness when he yelled out to the county's academy coach David Ripley. 'This man wants to meet Winston Davis. Do you have his number?' Wendell said in a typical West Indian accent. My heart skipped a beat considering this was said loud and clear right in front of several story-hungry touring journalists. 'Later, Wendell, later,' I stressed, but Wendell could not understand my fear. However, this was no Watergate scoop to be so wary of. Ripley said he would try and pass on the number after finishing his net duties.

I made my way to the souvenir shop and exchanged pleasantries with the store manager. I spotted a DVD on Davis and promptly bought it. After a few more purchases, the manager promised she would try and get Davis' number for me, but she could not provide any assurance.

Later that afternoon, I got a call from Ripley, who provided me Davis' number. Wary of interrupting his siesta, I thought it best to speak to Davis later. I could not wait for afternoon to turn to evening.

Davis agreed to be interviewed and said I could come the next day. Travelling to Bewdley, which is in another county—Worcestershire—was going to be a very costly affair. The journey had to be undertaken by road because train travel would eat into our time. I had to keep an eye on the India vs Northampton game, too. Talk about multi-tasking.

My fellow journalist Debasish Datta was keen on coming to meet Davis. We watched the Davis DVD to complete our preparation. How were we going to handle the sight of a neck-down paralysed fast bowler, it was our challenge. For Debasish, it would be more stark since he had seen Davis in his prime years.

Anna, a Monica Seles look-alike, answered the doorbell. We walked into a small and tidy house and there was Davis in his wheelchair welcoming us with a smile. Davis (fifty-three) was neatly dressed and wore thick leather shoes. He even smiled and laughed in typical West Indian style.

He moved around in his wheelchair, which had a golf ball as a knob to navigate the room. He remembered his 1983-84 and 1987-88 tours to India. 'I remember we used to get invited to parties and as soon as you stepped in at 8 p.m., you were asked, "what will you drink?" I used to be amazed because I wanted to know what I could get to eat. I was sharpening my teeth for some food but there was no food served till 10 p.m.,' he chuckled.

Photo frames of his playing days adorned the walls, the most prominent being one with fellow pacemen on the 1983-84 tour to India—Andy Roberts, Michael Holding, Wayne Daniel, Malcolm Marshall and Eldine Baptiste. My mind went back to October 1983 when Davis was one of the bowlers Gavaskar hit all over the park at Delhi's Feroz Shah Kotla to notch up his twenty-ninth Test century, putting him on par with Sir Don Bradman's tally.

His memory did not fail him about his seven-wicket burst against the Aussies in 1983. 'I was not supposed to play that game at Leeds. I was told of my inclusion on the morning of the match when Malcolm Marshall was injured. My first five overs went for thirty-five runs. I was hammered by David Hookes and Kim Hughes and then Clive Lloyd changed my end. Once I got the ball where I wanted to, they (Australians) did not have a clue.' In only his second one-day international, Davis took six of the last seven wickets, conceding only fourteen runs.

We were served tea by his assistant Anna. He could not even lift a cup and the sight of her feeding him was pitiable. The same arm that famously fractured England batsman Paul Terry in the Manchester Test of 1984 (the batsman returned to bat one-handed later in the innings to help Allan Lamb get a hundred) now could not hold a cup of tea.

But Davis refused to go down the road of self-pity. 'People come to me and ask, "how you coping" and I say, "I am not coping, I am living". You go from crying to living,' he says. He recalls the early days after the accident: 'I cried everyday...everyday. I used to bawl like a cow. I believe God used my tears to wash away my sorrows. Can I test that scientifically? No, but I believe that.'

A few months before the accident, he renewed his relationship with God. In church one day, he responded to the call of being close to God again. He headed towards the altar and made his peace with the Almighty.

'In November, 1997, I went up a mango tree to cut a branch but I was struck at the back of my head by another branch which was entangled with this branch. The blow I received at the back of the head was a tremendous one (the scar left its mark). My neck was broken there and I got paralysed neck down. We were clearing the land to build a church which is yet to be erected,' he recalls.

The irony of his renewed faith and the accident is taken well: 'Remember, God is good.' A message board in his living room states: 'ONE DAY AT A TIME. SHOW ME THE STAIRWAY I HAVE TO CLIMB. LORD, FOR MY SAKE, TEACH ME TO TAKE ONE DAY AT A TIME.'

Davis married an English lady, whom he had met in Australia on his 1984 tour there. She lived in Bewdley before moving to a nearby town. Through his stint at Northamptonshire, Davis settled down in England and has played first-class cricket in Australia and New Zealand.

Mark Ray, his captain at Tasmania during the 1985-86 season, recalls: 'During my four years with Tasmania in the Sheffield Shield, we had four West Indian-born fast bowlers: the peerless Michael Holding, the volatile and then inexperienced Patrick Patterson, the gentlemanly Neil Williams, who died far too young, and Winston.

'Winnie did a very professional job that season. He knew he had to get a wicket or two with the new ball then come back during the day to bowl tight spells, maintaining pressure on batsmen in often tough conditions—flat pitches and hot weather.

'He did all this with a no-fuss attitude that was greatly appreciated.

'He used his height with the new ball to attack the batsmen, and in his spells his variety and ability to hit the seam kept batsmen guessing.

'In the half a dozen games in which I captained him, Winnie never complained, tried as hard as he could and when I needed an extra over from him in a tight corner he took the ball and always said something along the lines of "no problem, skipper".

'On and off the field he was always able to find something to laugh about and that made him a very popular teammate.'

He asked Anna to give him some water. 'I do all the things I can do. What I can't do, I have people to help me for,' he said. The tilting wheelchair worked on a car battery.

When Davis wants to move around, he pushes the golf ball knob with his right hand forward. When he wants to sit back, he pushes the ball to another direction. He won't call the wheelchair his best friend. 'It is a useful tool. It helps me.'

'Things like this give you a certain amount of independence,' he says. 'If I was sitting in a normal chair and if I wanted to move, someone would have to come and move me. With this chair, I can go up and down. I go for my "walks" in the wheelchair. When I tell people I go for walks, they look at me (in shock). But I go for my walks in my wheelchair.'

He did not complain when he could not name any former teammate who dropped in to visit him. 'When I went home, I saw the guys I played with. England is a different society. I am not always here,' he says.

'I have a busy life. I am involved with the Worcester County Council, working with groups of people with disability. I am on various committees to ensure affected people are looked after.' Handling the financial front was a problem, but Davis did not make a big deal about it. Getting money for his treatment was a big worry when he suffered the body blow. He had retired from the county circuit and, in those days, there was no cricketers' association like there is in England now. Also, it is never easy when one is not an England player.

Cricket writer Engel wrote a piece in *The Guardian* about Davis' plight, and readers were encouraged to donate money for his treatment. Around 34,000 pounds were raised and the Winston Davis Trust got formed. 'To live with a disability in the UK is not cheap. It is very challenging. But there are government schemes set up so people like me can apply and receive help,' he says. His attitude towards money is: 'Money is a tool to be used to get the things you use in life.'

We were back to cricket talk. He was in the reserves when West Indies lost the 1983 World Cup final to India. 'Lloyd made some bad decisions, like reshuffling the batting order. That might have communicated the wrong spirit. I saw a grown man crying after the loss but I am not going to tell you who. It was a match we thought we should have won,' he said.

It saddened him that West Indies are not the force they used to be. 'It is not that they don't have talented players, but the attitude has changed. For me, attitude is everything. Poor management at the Board level and the players' attitude have contributed to the disintegration. Money can corrupt you. We always had the grouses and grunts but the team I played in, there was an unspoken understanding that this was bigger than cricket. We will not be an economic power like the US. We were a sporting power. We were known for our sporting prowess. When we came into town, people knew we were in town.'

Davis has come a long way since the accident. 'I don't think I got anything back. But I have gotten stronger, both physically and mentally,' he says. 'Let's put it like this—you can do a lot of things with a computer, you can discover new uses of it and that is what happens with me. I have met people similar to me and they are still carrying their burden.'

As I prepared to leave, he displayed his positive attitude yet again: 'God has given me peace. I don't lie on my bed thinking about what I have lost. When I wake up, I cannot wait to get out of bed. Some people stay in bed. I want to be able to do things. God has given me the chance to do that.

'The day will come when God will pull me out of this wheelchair and I will walk again.'

I approach the door to make my exit but Debasish is still in the living room. I can hear Debasish crying as he says goodbye.

Our hearts broke to leave him alone. Would anyone visit him again? But Davis is a tough man. And we would like to believe in the adage, threadbare though it is from overuse: Tough times don't last but tough people do.

Postscript

Winston Davis' international fast-bowling career coincided with the West Indies' dominance of world cricket. His seven wickets for fifty-one runs in the 1983 World Cup match against Australia at Leeds was no fluke, but he got an opportunity to play due to fellow paceman Malcolm Marshall being indisposed. Breaking into the great quartet of fast bowlers was a huge challenge, but the fact that he played in all six Tests against India in the 1983-84 series in India proves he enjoyed the faith of his captain, Clive Lloyd. Davis' otherwise limited opportunities fetched him forty-five wickets in fifteen Tests (eleven against India).

Clayton Murzello is *Mid-Day*'s Group Sports Editor. He has been covering cricket since 1988 and has reported from international cricket-playing countries like Australia, Bangladesh, England, South Africa, Sri Lanka, Zimbabwe and the UAE.

He is the recipient of two Sports Journalists' Federation of India (SJFI) awards for 'Excellence in Reporting and Writing'.

The Human Laboratory Called Eden

Mudar Patherya

> The vendor goes from stand to stand selling lime lozenges (*lebu lojenz*), extracting them from his glass jar with a spoon tied by a string to his jar and then putting the lozenge into a paper receptacle which he hands over to the customer.

India is the most emotional country in the world. Kolkata is its most temperamental city. And the Eden Gardens its most volatile showpiece.

Ergo! The Eden Gardens may be a cricket ground for all those who know cricket; it is a human laboratory for everyone else.

It has taken this fool more than four decades of 'observing' cricket at the Eden Gardens to realise that only a fool goes to the Eden Gardens to watch twenty-two performers; the intellectual goes to watch the 70,000.

Within this 70,000, there are a number of spectator species, their number peaking at thirty-six in the early 1980s and now declining to about twenty-two (some recorded here).

The any-team, any-season Kolkatan: This species works in a bank, earns ₹18,375 including dearness allowance, saves ₹3,457 after paying his life insurance premium and probably spends more than ₹1,250 on his 'season' ticket (validity only for the Test match). He sets up his annual winter routine after the BCCI announces the itinerary. Watches every session of every Test match day. Why? Because he has been doing so since Kanhai scored 256 in 1958-59; any day missed would be an interruption of an existing tradition that he proudly showcases in *para* (neighbourhood) arguments: 'Not since I saw the West Indies…' His nemesis was the former Chief Minister, Siddhartha Shankar Ray, who watched every Test match since Jardine's MCC in 1933-34 and died in 2011. Since then our friend has been breathing easier.

The temperamental Kolkatan: Our friend comes to the ground with his opinion on his collar button. When the Australian Services Team came to play East Zone in 1945, the police fired on protesting students (killing one). Our temperamental friend and his friends cornered the players and 'demanded' a minute's silence for the deceased. Then when the media reported that the wristy Mushtaq Ali had been dropped on the eve of the 'Test', he led another agitation with this demand: 'No Mushtaq, no Test'. The word went back to the police that things could get out of hand. Ditto to the selectors. Quietly, Mushtaq Ali was drafted in. At one point when the agitators trooped into the ground and took the visiting Australians by surprise, the quick-thinking Lindsay Hassett asked one of them for a cigarette and another for a matchstick. The latter fumbled; another did the same; within minutes a dozen were scampering for strikes for *'Meester Hazziit'*—and the agitation was effectively defused.

The recorder-of-history Kolkatan: The Kolkatan is no mere spectator;

he is a recorder of history. His word will be passed down to his son who will pass it down to his son (which explains why the legend of Shibdas Bhaduri's Mohun Bagan taking on the East Yorkshire Regiment in 1911 is still being analysed in the bylanes of North Calcutta). Soon it will be one great-grandfather's word against another's. As an extension of this, when the batsmen in the middle add only thirty-four runs between lunch and tea, he will tell you that this had happened in an Eden Gardens Test in the late 1940s. Which explains why he will come ninety minutes before the match starts to watch the nets; when he goes back home he will consume twenty-five dinner table-minutes to explain Bedi's loop at nets or how Boycott batted to Willis on a side pitch. After the match, he will be off in a flash to stand as close as he can to the Club House gate to see the players walk into the bus, so that he may be able to go back and tell his awestruck Hooghly district audience, 'Imran looked at me from the team bus when I waved at him.'

The anything-for-a-cricketer Kolkatan: If you want adulation from a Mumbaikar, make more money than anyone else. You want a Delhiite to fall at your feet, move into Race Course Road. You want a Kolkatan to worship you for life, swing a bat better than anyone else. I quote Mushtaq Ali: 'After the day's play at Eden Gardens, I left the pavilion and went back to my hosts' place, when I discovered that my wrist watch was missing. The most I could remember was that I had held it in my hand, while I started leaving the pavilion, intending, of course, to put it on. Anxiously, I took a taxi and came back to the Eden Gardens, all along to check up if I had left in the dressing room by mistake. As it was not there, I came out of the pavilion gate and intended having a last look to see if I might have dropped it outside, while obliging fans and shaking hands before entering the car. As is customary for all big matches, a small crowd of fans still lingered there. Hardly had I begun my search, when a young man stepped forward and asked me if I had dropped my watch. He produced it immediately from his closed fist with the remark, "Here it is, Mr Mushtaq Ali".'

The participating Kolkatan: The Kolkata spectator is not someone who goes to watch; he goes to influence the match. When Tony Greig stood between India and a first innings MCC collapse in 1976-77, he took his perch behind long off and fished out a mirror which he shone into Greig's eyes (he put it into his bag only when Greig got down on his knees, hands folded, requesting him to stop). When Kapil Dev would run in to bowl, he would start his 'appeal' even before the ball had been bowled. When Kapil started his run, he would commence an orchestrated chorus of just one word: 'Out!' (pronounced 'Aaaaaoooooooouuuuuuut!'). Multiply this by 70,000. As soon as the ball passed the bat, he checked two things—if the ball passed to the wicketkeeper, the sound evaporated like a stock market crash, but if the ball snicked or hit the wicket, then that sound became a human thunder that rolled across at least 5 km to the Exide stop on Chowringhee, where corporate types would immediately turn on their televisions saying, 'Definitely *kichhu hoyechhey…dekhi!* (Definitely something has happened, let us see)'. The loudest sound ever heard on a cricket field anywhere in the world. Surprisingly no one measures crowds for decibel records.

The better-beware-of-my-anger Kolkatan: The Kolkata spectator is a demanding, paying public. If there is something he doesn't like, he hoots. If there is something he absolutely abhors, he gets physical. In 1966, when the Cricket Association of Bengal overprinted tickets and thousands of spectators had no seats, they spilled into the ground. Finally, when there was no space left on the boundary edge either, they could take it no more; so one of them burnt the hessian awning covering the stands. When one of them remonstrated with the police for lobbing a tear gas shell into the stands, he was beaten up. Then the spectators could take it no longer. Sure, they burnt chairs, stands and hunted officials who had encashed on the black market. At no point was any of the ire directed at the players who were terrified all right; the great Charlie Griffith ran to the Great Eastern Hotel and when one of the spectators offered him safe passage in a vehicle, he ran even faster (meanwhile, All India Radio went off the air with a one-word excuse, 'fog'). There were other times when he lost his cool: when Gavaskar lashed at everything from the word go and threw his wicket away under Kapil Dev's captaincy against the West Indies in 1983 and India lost the Test without a fight, the spectators emptied their banana peels on him (some also hit his wife) and SMG—Sunil Manohar Gavaskar—swore never to play in Kolkata again. The other occasion when he lost his marbles was when India lost the semi-final to Sri Lanka in 1996—again without a fight. What did the rest of India do? Editors wrote polite copy and said, 'How badly we had played' and television viewers tsk-tsked and switched off their sets. The Eden spectators were the only ones to have said, 'This stinks!' The only way the spectators could have got themselves heard was by throwing in whatever they could get: PET water bottles, bananas and oranges. Then there was this instance when Tendulkar was given run out against Pakistan when he was clearly in (replays showed!) and the spectators torched every single newspaper they could find in the stands and what did they get? The next day, the remainder of the match was played without a single spectator. It is because of this kind of protest that the third umpire has become a consistent reality, but does anyone thank the Eden spectators for this?

The long-suffering Kolkatan: The Eden species has struggled to survive. If he is not attached to a club, he doesn't get a ticket. If there is no public sale of tickets, he has to beg or borrow. If there is a public sale then it is usually routed through a lottery, meaning that he has to buy a coupon for 25 paise, each coupon with a one in a hundred chance of winning the right to buy a match ticket. On the rare occasion when tickets were actually sold across the counter—as during the India-Australia Test in 1969-70—that was so badly managed that six died in a stampede while doing nothing more adventurous than queuing up for tickets—7,000 tickets for 20,000 who turned up. The spectators have to take much of the sun across the day, can't take water in any longer; the food they get in the stalls under the stands is inedible; for years, bums on concrete hurt; the toilets stink and for some strange reason it is virtually impossible to get a mobile call in or out of the stands (which means that folks at home have to keep praying that you have survived the ordeal). Why go there at all, people ask? Because sir, Eden Gardens is in the *'blaad'*.

The I-embrace-all Kolkatan: You may call the Eden spectator temperamental and he won't mind. But you call him communal or parochial or jingoistic and he will do a sit-down protest shouting 'Inquilab Zindabad'. His argument: Didn't we applaud Waqar Hasan on every delivery as an encouragement for him to get his century (he got out at ninety-seven, more nervous with the applause, but that is another story)? Didn't we protest (along with the Naxalites) for the anonymous Asian when we discovered that the Australian Doug Walters had served during the Vietnam war? Didn't we turn up—all 85,000—to watch England play Australia in a World Cup final? Didn't we applaud Tony Greig's MCC victory over India in 1976-77, that resulted in a rare victory lap by a visiting team around the stadium? Didn't we give Asif Iqbal a standing ovation while he was walking back after he had announced his retirement in 1979-80, reducing the batsman to tears?

The I-am-not-really-a-reporter-but-I-just-have-to-be-there Kolkatan: This is the story of yet another waster turned cricket writer: 'I am a casual writer. But when a big Test match is coming, all I need to do is to write to my friend at *Paris Match* or *Der Speigel* and ask whether they would be interested in seeing a piece on cricket with no obligation to print. Of course, all they have to do is send a letter by fax to the Cricket Association of Bengal (CAB) asking for media accreditation. If the CAB gets 1000 such applications, it is their problem. All I know is that once I get the accreditation, I can walk in with *'thaat'*, the swagger of the privileged, into the Club House, saunter into the press box (with everybody wondering who the hell he is), demand my free lunch box, watch the press box television rather than see some fellows scampering 200 yards away, leave at three, see the first two days for novelty, never bother to go again and tell the fellows sitting in Europe, "It was nothing worth writing about for your great paper".'

The I-go-to-a-festival Kolkatan: I am the Kolkatan who tries to raise a laugh wherever I am with the objective of beating the gloom and making the world a better place to be in. And I go to the Eden Gardens for just one reason: Where else will I get an audience as large as this? I go there for another reason as well: on television, you can always call in Sidhu between the overs to raise a laugh, but what about the poor spectators? Who can regale their spirits when things are dull in the middle? So I have my usuals: when a portly non-Bengali walks in with his wife and cushion, my standard wisecrack is: *'Ki boudi, ranna time-y shesh holo aajkey?'* (What sister, lunch cooked on time today?) When a grotesque gent walks in with a hat, coat, muffler, dark glasses and mega binoculars hanging around his neck, my line, *'Kobey chharlo?* (When were you released?)' has the entire stand in splits. Then there was the time, I turned Zubin Mehta: *'Bhai-era boneyra! Chup-chaap keno? Chitkaar korun, chitkaar korun!* (Brothers and sisters, why are you so quiet? Raise a noise, raise a noise!),' I invoked like a professional conductor, with my back to the match. The third man couldn't figure it out; the batsman was defending ball after ball and 10,000 spectators behind him were having their time of the afternoon. Nowadays every Eden Gardens ticket has this warning imprinted on the back: 'Please do not bring bugles, etc., and play on them inside the stadium as that creates a bad impression on the foreign team.' Cricket-watching RIP.

I go-there-for-the-quaintness Kolkatan: I go to the Eden Gardens because it is still a world in a time warp (thank god). The vendor who goes from stand to stand selling lime lozenges (*lebu lojenz*), extracting them from his glass jar with a spoon tied by the rope to his jar and then putting the lozenge into a paper receptacle which he hands over to the customer. The vendor who goes from stand to stand hawking a '*khelar maath spesal* (playground special)' tabloid which has been printed only to commemorate the match with pictures of the players, exciting every young kid to pester his parent with '*Ekta kiney deenna!* (Buy me one, no?).' This is the mofussil in a world gone modern. One of these days, *National Geographic* will send its cameraman to an Eden Test.

I go-there-for-the-characters Kolkatan: The Eden Gardens during a Test match represents the biggest collection of characters you can get in a public event anywhere in India. There is Rahman the scorer in the club house, who could be heard two stands away. They forbade him from speaking while an over was in progress on the ground that it would shatter the batsman's concentration. Cricket writer Scyld Berry describes him: 'Rahman brings to his chore of reading out the bowling figures the zeal of Demosthenes. Like the best orators he stands up while his disciples sit clustered around him; in the left hand, he holds a book, with the relevant notes on which to base his discourse. At significant moments he stabs the air with his right forefinger...his voice is metallic and staccato, not just faintly so, but to the extent that it is one of the few noises in creation that could make machine-gun fire sound like sweet music...what Rahman says when he rises to his feet and stabs the air is "bowling, bowling", the analysis of the various bowlers. But in Rahman's strident Indian English it comes out as "bolling! bolling!" Then there is the spectator who would be seen at the same corner of the same stand match after match, year after year. One day his perch was vacant; when he entered really late, someone asked him. He said: *'Chheley maara gelo. Puriye diye aschi. Ektuderi hoyegelo!* (Son died, just cremated him, got a little late).' It actually happened.

The-I-had-to-be-there-because-I-got-it-for-free Kolkatan: This is the story of yet another spectator, 'I am an income tax officer. I don't have much of an interest in cricket. I go to the Test match because I get tickets free from assessees whose cases are stuck with me. I never quite ask for tickets, I only casually say, "See if you have and no one is going…" but they get the idea. I usually get about five, but I choose the one closest to the Club House. There is something about being able to say "L1", which means that not only could I see what was the colour of Prosenjit's shorts during his thirteen-minute visit but I could talk with authority on whether Tendulkar's lbw was really out or not.'

The I-go-there-for-the-family-spirit Kolkatan: The Eden Gardens came closest to a collective picnic for the Kolkatan, where the spectator could soak in the mellow sun, eat sandwiches from his hamper, burp on his lunch as early as noon, extract precious *gorom cha* (warm tea) from a flask nestled inside his cane basket, share the oranges/binoculars with his new-found neighbours and create an impromptu family two rows up and two rows down (dare anyone sitting in another part of the block say anything about the seventy people in his 'territory'). It was Facebook in the open even before Facebook was created, except now that Facebook has indeed been created, the police have banned taking food, fruit or binoculars into the ground. Irony.

Postscript

The what-do-I-know-about-cricket-Kolkatan: A new spectator species has been spotted at the Eden Gardens. She is nineteen years old. Is attending her first IPL match because, 'It is in the evening under lights, there is music, everything will be over in three hours, this is more fun than being at a multiplex—and there is an outside chance that I will get to see Shah Rukh Khan in flesh and blood 200 metres away.' She is an enthusiastically bobbing speck in the middle of a Mexican wave, she cheers mishits for four, she couldn't be bothered who wins as long the number of sixes per match exceeds twenty and she is proud to state that she cannot name more than four players from either side thirty minutes after the match. Her phrase is: 'ideology neutral'.

Mudar Patherya was one of those incurables who attended the last morning of the India-England Test match with 75,000 others when it was imminent that India would lose within forty-five minutes. If this does not indicate his mental balance, consider that he wrote cricket for a living for a decade even as his classmates completed their MBAs, extended into the stock market thereafter to earn a stable salary, then started an annual reports consultancy with no experience, now cleans the streets, parks and lakes of Kolkata for a living and is still crazy enough to sit out at the Eden Gardens in 38°C to celebrate the return of KKR following its IPL victory.

The Batwallahs

Sharda Ugra

> There is another tale of a fast bowler, Fayaz Ahmed from Baramulla/Sopore, who didn't turn up after one average season in the mid-90s. Fayaz, they say, '*paar chala gaya* (went across the border)', local euphemism for picking up the gun.

Who knows what they made of Danish Ahsan, as he walked to keep pace with the arrival of dawn. They would surely have seen him, the men with the guns on both sides of the Valley's barbed wire divide. The teenager would set off at four every morning, the soft tap of his footsteps the only sound on the quiet road from Dialagam to Anantnag. As he walked, village dirt tracks gave way to tarmac, the canopy of blue velvet melted into comforting first light and inky shadows and shapes revealed themselves as rice fields, poplars and checkposts.

To those he went past, he could have been a wastrel, wanderer, runaway or even a rogue but the boy with the bright eyes and tireless legs was only a practical dreamer. He was not about to let distance—or unreliable transport—get in the way of his reaching the landscape of his dreams: a rundown sports ground in Anantnag hidden off a market street.

By 6.30 a.m. every morning for a month, Danish would be there, hurrying his pace just a little, dodging past the Sumo taxis noisily rolling into their stand searching for morning customers. That long walk from village to field, that everyday act of faith, was over but Danish's personal odyssey had only begun. Along with two-hundred-odd other boys, he would change out of his dusty home clothes into his carefully preserved white shirt and trousers, lace up his shoes and for a few hours become someone else: that most unexpected of natives, the Kashmiri cricketer.

At the Anantnag ground, the talent search camp has concluded and it is match day for the Under-14s, Under-16s and Under-19s that have been selected to go one step further. Danish is among them, milling about easily with boys taller than him by a head as well as those who reach his armpits. It's Friday, the *khutba* (religious narration) is ringing out from the mosque that overlooks the ground. There is a crowd watching the swirl of whites from the banked stands overgrown with grass; a motley mix of an electrician and school teacher watch with a detached look as they wait for the afternoon *azaan* that will call them for prayer. The officials supervising the matches exchange shrugs about missing the Friday *namaz* and in the next instant are barking orders at their charges.

Anantnag district captain, the tall and burly Ghulam Rasool, had once rushed over to a mosque with a bunch of cricketers all still in their whites. The puzzled congregation looked at each other and the whisper went around, '*Yeh kaun si jamaat ke hain*? (Which sect is this?)' Rasool remembers replying, '*Hum batwaale hain* (We're the batwallahs).'

It is both incongruous and organic, this open acknowledgement of two varying faiths. Cricket in Kashmir is itself incongruous, something frivolous in a place which has lost both its frivolity and its innocence. Tourists may have returned but the Valley is no carefree holiday destination, it could perhaps never be. Its lush beauty extracts a price both from those who live off it, watch over it and those who come merely to feast.

The human spirit is but a plaything here, it could soar one instant and be shredded in the next. Normalcy in Kashmir is not a condition, it's actually conditionality.

But in Kashmir's open spaces where this complex, silly game is played, the air somehow feels slightly altered. It blows through the Sher-e-Kashmir Stadium in Srinagar and its decaying, blackened bleachers; over the narrow strip of mud near a Jhelum backwater outside Norbel, where Osman strikes a crisp on-drive which ends up under mulberry bushes; it rustles the striped pyjamas of a boy watching from a cliffside as Mars XI take on Wonder Boys XI on Seer's spectacular new ground cut high into a hillside.

Cricket in Kashmir lives in its own time zone. When the rest of the country's season ends, Kashmir's begins; as others curse the heat in Mumbai and Chennai, Kashmir's cricketers swarm into the Polo ground, the university's play fields and onto disused golf courses. It is proof enough that the game has survived. Through climate changes of the heart and the mind, through an extended off season of uncertainty and violence, through the optimism of its young and the doggedness of its old.

In Srinagar, when the Jammu & Kashmir Cricket Association (JKCA) decided to open up their ground, the Sher-e-Kashmir Stadium, after a seven-year freeze, it took twenty workers four months in 1996 to clear the four feet high grass and, like expeditioners in salwars, finally unearth the playing square. The Srinagar Club League which was quietly re-initiated then involved only fifteen-sixteen clubs. Today, there are sixty formal teams in the Srinagar League with a new system of a divisional ladder taking vague shape.

In Anantnag, Abdul Qayuum, the most successful fast bowler from the state ('he was as fast as Srinath', the locals say), and everyone who has anything to do with cricket in the region, is pitching in. Mohammed Shafi, opening batsman for the J&K Ranji team is on umpiring duty along with Sajid Nisar, who represented the state in the Under-17s and Under-19s. They end up umpiring and coaching at the same time, correcting batsmen's footwork and bowlers' follow-throughs.

Mushtaq Ahmed, who played inter-university and reached the state trials keeps the order, is heading off to procure the boy's lunch of samosas and bananas with Rasool. Ahmed lost his young son in an accident at home and comes to the cricket 'because I think of these boys as my seven-year-old'.

The sentiment and energy to be found in Kashmir's scattered cricket grounds is tangible but, to the outsider, utterly inexplicable. There are only a couple of turf wickets in the state, there is little expert coaching to be found outside of Srinagar, there is no established league in place, the game can only be played between April and September, out of sync with the rest of India's cricket. Only once in its history has the J&K team got beyond the first round of the Ranji Trophy. Role models are thin on the ground and despite the best contortions of the BCCI's selection committee, no player from the state has ever represented India.

For the state's cricketers, these are trifles. Soldiers and sandbags are part of the landscape. Every time they enter the 'home ground', the stunning but decaying Sher-e-Kashmir which stands across the chief minister's private office, local players have to show their special ID cards and submit kit bags and stand in queue for a security check. Hemmed in by insanity and inhumanity in Kashmir, cricket's mythology is re-invented, its fussy rituals given a new layer of meaning.

Remember, uncertainty in Kashmir is rarely glorious so cricket represents an order, a rootedness, sanity even. The Central Reserve Police Force (CRPF) has been camping in the Sher-e-Kashmir stadium for the last fifteen years and its 60th battalion has taken over the pavilion building; boxes of ammunition are now stored in the old dressing rooms. Among the permitted spectators at a JKCA league game is an assault-rifle-wielding CRPF jawan who watches the match from inside his guard post that faces the field.

Still, the players first change into whites under a tired scoreboard and a towering ring of six-storey high chinars. Still, bowlers swivel around on their heels and holler 'how's that?' at the umpires, who are just young men in lab coats that reach their knees. A no-ball is still a no-ball and if you're going back to one that snakes through straight, that's out. Progress here is measured in Eliot-esque coffee spoons.

Srinagar held its first Ranji Trophy match after a sixteen-year-gap last season. So what if the visiting Odisha team and even the lunch packs had to be frisked at the gate? So what if no Kashmiri had played for the country? When the MRF Pace Foundation held a talent scouting camp with former India bowlers TA Sekhar and Javagal Srinath in attendance, 400 boys turned up. Fast bowler Abid Nabi became the first J&K player to be picked for the North Zone team in the Deodhar Trophy and even bowled at India's finest at the nets in Mohali before the Test against England. His name was uttered across the state with a hopeful echo until he joined the ICL.

In Gulmarg, a local family strolling on the meadows hears the word cricket from the outsiders and wants to know if Nabi will play for India. In Seer, two hours from the capital, a village boy randomly declares, 'Abid Nabi is in Srinagar today,' as if the superstar of Kashmiri cricket had just called to keep us all informed.

In the backdrop of cricket's time-stopping qualities, it is easy to assume that the generation of players which grew up during the height of insurgency in Kashmir lived like cricketers in the rest of the country do, immune to political turmoil, cut off from the world, obsessed in their universe. They did but they really didn't.

'My father put me in cricket for two reasons,' says Sajid Nisar. 'One, to keep away from the smoking-drinking crowd and, second, to ensure I stayed away from militancy.' The survivors from those days insist that the militants didn't directly affect the game or its players but their footprints are never far away. Shafi spent many summers on the field when cricket and the curfew seemed made for each other. Boys would be out of their houses early before the curfew fell and spend the day on the playing field of Nilandrous outside Anantnag.

When the shops opened for a few hours in the evening, it was time for the players to head home. They were, it seemed, the only free people in the neighbourhood. The under-currents of such a blithe existence were never too far away. When Shafi was picked for the state junior team for the national Under-17 championship, the militants had already put out notices in newspapers forbidding local boys from representing J&K in any competition outside the state. Batting for J&K juniors would have put his family in danger. Shafi stayed at home. He says today in his gentle, most matter-of-fact voice, 'Those are the best years of a cricketer's life, aren't they?'

There is another tale of a fast bowler, Fayaz Ahmed from Baramulla/Sopore, who didn't turn up after one average season in the mid-90s. Fayaz, they say, '*paar chala gaya* (went across the border)', local euphemism for picking up the gun. He is believed to have died a violent death, killed by the army—whether as a militant or innocent victim is not certain.

Khursheed A Tarzan, director of Physical Education and Sports, University of Kashmir, says, 'They didn't even find his body...we went and gave his blazer to his mother. Lots of children…we don't know where they went.' His office window overlooks the dome of the Hazratbal Mosque and the university's cricket ground where the Mirza Nooruddin Memorial knockout tournament is on.

The event, now in its sixth year run by the Amateur Cricket Club (ACC), is deliberately different from the besieged proceedings at the Sher-e-Kashmir. The folks at ACC want to be the ones to take fresh guard: the university has given them a three-year run at organising cricket as well as the space to lay five new turf wickets in an adjoining field. The state's traditional forte in the game is the fast bowler and, naturally, the batsman who can face them. Yet cricket in the state comes across as loaded with little else but possibility.

Football is traditionally the state's No 1 sport and J&K's Mehrajuddin Wadoo plays mid-field for the national football team. But everyone knows what could have happened if one day Nabi had been tossed the new ball for India.

What does it all stack up to? What does cricket in Kashmir mean, to the game as it stands? It is unfair for Abid Nabi to have to do what the government cannot, but as Kashmir's cricket comes out of a long winter, all it can do is good.

When asked what their cricket needs are, Abdul Rauf, a former Ranji player and now joint secretary J&K sports council, says, '*Sab kuch* (Everything)'. Legend has it that Rauf could clear the chinars around the Sher-e-Kashmir with his sixes. Qayuum, who in 2002 led J&K to the knock out stage of the Ranji Trophy for the only time in its history (only to be replaced the following season), says Kashmir's cricketers need to play more matches outside the state, need invitations to tournaments like the Buchi Babu and the Moin-ud-Dowla. ACC's Mansoor Ahmed says it needs teams from the rest of India to play fixtures during the summer. It could all happen.

Whether it is Danish, all-rounder Pervez Rasool who plays for the state's Under-19 team or nineteen-year-old Raees Ahmed Nedaf from Lahripura near Pahalgam, the state's young cricketers have a common past: learning the game through watching Doordarshan's much mocked live telecasts of India matches; re-learning their batting skills when confronted by the rare, turf wicket and working out how to read top quality spin.

When he was an active cricketer, Nisar bought cricket DVDs featuring his favourites: Andy Flower, Matthew Hayden and Sourav Ganguly. 'You know Dravid's cover drive? I want to hit the ball like that,' Nedaf, batting at No 3 for Lahripura, says. When they run into any kind of formal coaching, the key turns in the lock and the boys find themselves staring at what seem like riches. Danish has learnt about using his top hand and tells how, suddenly and miraculously, he can control his shots better.

Within the formal structures the heroes, in descending order of age, are Sachin Tendulkar, Rahul Dravid, Virender Sehwag, Irfan Pathan and MS Dhoni, some choosing to pair Sehwag off with Shahid Afridi, who they think of as a cross-border twin. On the street leading to Srinagar's iconic Lal Chowk, the vendors do not stock up on posters of Tendulkar and the rest; it's mostly of the boys from across the border.

On Sundays, recreational players in the maidans of Srinagar and Tangmarg are spotted wearing the coloured uniforms of Pakistan, Australia and strangely even New Zealand, but not India's blue and yellow. The teacher in Tangmarg whose team is wearing the Pakistani shirts says apologetically, 'You know how it is in the shops...the boys couldn't find anything else.' In Nilandrous, one Sunday cricketer approaches, wanting to know whether anything will be written about politics and then demands to correct the illusion that the presence of cricket implies an absence of ground-level turmoil. He states that Kashmiris still want independence, but surely not from the game that keeps all of India agog.

The JKCA, you suspect, need some form of freedom from a long history of faction-fighting. Officials in Jammu and Kashmir have for long worked at cross purposes, so much so that two teams landed up to play one game. 'We are stuck in litigation all the time...our house has never been in order,' says one official. Srinagar's local league is not advertised or publicised in the papers for fear of the rival group in the city taking the ruling powers of the association to court and holding up the games.

After the fixtures are made, clubs are informed by phone a few days before their games and told to turn up. JKCA's share of the gym equipment sent out by the cash-rich BCCI to every state association is lying unused, even as there is talk of building a new stadium using president Farooq Abdullah's contacts. Mansoor Ahmed, attached to the ACC and also Nabi's coach, is delighted at the location of the new turf wickets at the university. They will be next to the Dal Lake and, he says, the breeze off the Dal will help the ball to swing.

It is perhaps the way to go: to leave the gorgeous Sher-e-Kashmir ground to the CRPF and its fate. To understand that if the game must go on in this beautiful, blighted landscape, those inside it must think outside its boundaries and those outside it must understand the Kashmiri cricketer's depth of feeling and his strength of will.

Postscript

This article was written in 2006 when *India Today* sent me to the Kashmir Valley to see how cricket, India's most-loved sport, was played and perceived in a state where the issue of national identity remains trapped between political compulsions and individual argument. Cricket was fighting its good fight in Kashmir and it was a stirring stuff to write about.

Five years on, while Indian cricket has transformed into a multi-million-dollar behemoth, cricket in Kashmir finds itself still isolated, cut off from the mainstream. No wider use is made of an excellent summer season in the Valley by the rest of Indian cricket, even though Farooq Abdullah heads JKCA and serves on the BCCI as the head of its marketing committee.

Kashmir's cricketers are left adrift once the summer is over, cut off from the change bubbling through the rest of India. Infrastructure for coaching and training in the Valley is still paltry, even though the BCCI's handouts to states have skyrocketed since the creation of the IPL. One of the boys in the story says things have improved over the last five years, 'but in terms of the quality of the cricket we play, it's only by ten per cent'.

Maybe the arrival of Bishen Singh Bedi as Ranji coach can be Kashmir's catalyst. If talent is left untapped because things are being badly run he will, we can be sure, let us all know.

Sharda Ugra is Senior Editor, ESPNCricinfo. She has been a sports journalist for more than twenty years, having worked for *Mid-Day* in Mumbai, national broadsheet *The Hindu* in their Mumbai bureau and weekly news magazine *India Today* in Delhi before joining ESPNCricinfo, the world's biggest independent single-sport website.

Me, Doc and the BATboy

Sukhwant Basra

[I was wary of meeting Leander for I was a fan and I was afraid he would catch on and that, in turn, would compromise how he looked at me as a journalist. But Doc and I had always got along well. Soon Doc became my source for writing on Leander.]

Leander Paes first came to my attention when his name was three strokes away from mine in the draw of an Under-18 tournament in Calcutta. 'The BAT kid,' I remember thinking. In the first round I lost to a crafty local player called Anirban Dutta in three sets and with that I lost out on a chance to face the boy who would go on to win junior Wimbledon a year or so later. But Dutta had given Paes a tough time and I had given Dutta a torrid one. I remember thinking later that I might have had an outside chance to show the BAT kid with the fancy equipment (those were days when we used Bata Ultimos as tennis shoes and getting any kind of racquet was an exercise in cajoling and pestering relatives living abroad) a shot or two.

I was an idiot to quit tennis soon after! A decision I will regret all my life—after I saw the kind of work ethic many, who represented India, had.

As the years rolled on, I drifted through an MBA, mass communication and four failed attempts at the civil services exam. Crushed after the grind of my father's regimen while playing tennis and the mental squeeze of what is one of India's most sapping examinations, I was no longer looking for challenges. Writing came easy. Journalism, even easier. To this day, I am pleasantly surprised that someone is willing to pay me for watching and writing on tennis—a sport that seeped further into my soul when I coached for a period of seven years, while continuing to pursue my dreams in academia.

Through this time, I kept an eye on Leander's career. Strangely enough, I never looked up to any tennis player from abroad. Becker was always a treat to watch even though, in terms of work ethic, Ivan Lendl was closer to my heart. But there was no pressing desire to meet them or even see them in person. The only tennis player I admired was Leander Paes. After all, hadn't he come out of a system that beat so many of us? Did he not achieve the nigh impossible when many cowards like me gave up? Leander Paes fascinated me!

My association with the Paes' began far before I became a journalist. As a coach my friend Anurag and I were involved in the Chandigarh Lawn Tennis Association's (CLTA) Punwire programme which saw a lightweight like Chandigarh claim four national titles in the year 1999—the youngest ever men's hardcourt champion Sunil Kumar Sipaeya along with boys Under-18, Under-14 and a sub-junior doubles national title.

Looking to provide Sunil with the right launch pad for his foray into international tennis, CLTA began to weigh his options. In the end, the association chose to sign Sunil with Leander's father Dr Vece

Paes' fledgling sports management company Paes en Sport, while turning down the likes of International Management Group (IMG). I signed the contract on behalf of CLTA.

Doc began to visit Chandigarh often and I would stick to him like a leech whenever he visited, in an effort to unravel the secret to making another Leander. Doc was surprised when I met him as a journalist, for he thought I was really passionate about coaching. Except that as a coach I had to listen to IAS officers who knew nothing about the game as compared to me. It was not possible to take their inanities forever.

I was wary of meeting Leander for I was a fan and I was afraid he would catch on and that, in turn, would compromise how he looked at me as a journalist. But Doc and I had always got along well. Soon Doc became my source for writing on Leander. At times he would even give me quotes from his son while being a bit surprised at my reluctance to approach the man himself. I was writing for *The Times of India* at the time and given that paper's mammoth reach, it was only a matter of time before Leander had read some of my articles. He told me later that he was surprised and bemused at the intimate knowledge of his plans the journalist had while having never met him or even spoken to him. My source, of course, was impeccable—his father.

Then the time came when I had to speak to Leander directly. I was no longer content with doing the 'goodie-goodie' stories. I now needed quotes that Doc could no longer provide.

In 2001, the Indian Davis Cup team had not been paid its dues for a couple of years. I had the story. I got the others on record and called him to get his quotes. Leander has always been a crafty rascal. At the time, he appealed to the emotional side of me and asked for the story to be printed a few days later. He had wanted to talk to the All India Tennis Association (AITA) president himself before the matter hit the press. I went abroad for a week. By the time I came back, the federation had cleared all the dues of the players. My story was dead.

I berated myself for putting Leander before my job. I felt cheated of my little scoop. Over the next few months, the story became a minor irritant far back in memory. But Leander did not forget. Years on, he helped me with the moral support I needed to do some of my biggest tennis stories. He would not give me information, but he could not lie to me if I had it.

In a strange way, Leander has an elephant's memory. Strange! Because, he has an astounding ability to forget unpleasantness. I had ripped into his captaincy for playing the fifth rubber against Pakistan in the Davis Cup tie held at Mumbai. It was the odd discordant piece in a wave of jingoistic bull. He met me months later as if nothing had happened. I presumed he had not read it in the excitement of the birth of his daughter. Years later he told me he had read it and agreed with it except that he had no choice but to play.

Postscript

When I moved to Mumbai as Sports Editor of the *Hindustan Times*, hanging out with Leander became a regular feature when he flew back home for his breaks. He showed what seemed, to me, the shockingly wasteful lifestyles of the celeb lot and I took him for dosas to Matunga. He would be jetlagged and I, drinking. We spent a lot of time drinking together: me booze, him tea.

Leander now calls me 'beyond repair' for we have given up on each other in one crucial way: he does not tell me what to write, I don't try to guide him on being available for the media.

Sukhwant Basra is one of India's leading tennis correspondents. He has written extensively on the sport for *The Times of India* and *DNA*. At present, he is the national sports editor with the *Hindustan Times*. He misses the days of active reporting, far removed from the glorified foremanship that the editor's job usually devolves to.

Nightwatchman, for a Night

Sriram Dayanand

> Kallicharan had set about the Indian bowling with a dazzling century. It must have been dazzling, for he was being paid the ultimate Bangalore compliment by the admiring spectators that day: 'Bats just like a left-handed Viswa, doesn't he?' they smiled at each other knowingly.

It was a role reversal I couldn't have braced myself for. It felt like my very consciousness had been inverted. I had emerged out of a wormhole and now had a viewpoint that defied logic. The reversal was unimaginably dramatic. It was bound to be. But it was not anything I could have even dreamt of when I headed out to meet a friend for dinner at the Chinnaswamy Stadium.

It was a starry moonlit night in Bangalore. Dinner that night at the Karnataka State Cricket Association (KSCA) clubhouse had been a night for reminiscence and relentless cricket chatter. The years came flooding back as I sat with my friend on the steps of the pavilion, masquerading for the evening as an outdoor restaurant patio. The stadium, of course, was empty. The gargantuan light towers were mere silhouettes against the moonlit sky and the giant electronic scoreboard was just a sheet of black in the distance. Dim overhead lights shone in the stands, most of them bare, bereft of chairs or seats.

Out in the middle, even in the hazy illumination, you could spot the row of strips of earth that were the pitches. A rope barrier was strung out around them, demarcating the sanctum-sanctorum of the Chinnaswamy. The grass was an even lush green. Water sprinklers were busy all around, and we could hear their metronomic clatter as they bathed most of the turf in a haze of spray.

It was beautiful and surreal. And it was just about to get even more so. My supremely well-connected friend was busy, waving out to people at adjacent tables and exchanging greetings with passers-by—all of them a part of the cloistered membership rosters that such clubhouses foster diligently. As we sipped our beers, a gentleman stopped by our table to say hello to him. An official of the clubhouse, he shook my hand, welcomed me and enquired politely about the service before bidding us goodbye.

I turned my gaze back to the middle. The mind was awash with imagery and memories of events that were rooted there when my friend nudged me, smiled and asked, 'Do you want to go down to the middle and take a walk around the pitch?' The incredulous expression on my face surely sufficed as an answer, not that he needed one. He walked over to where the same official was standing and had a quick chat with him. I saw him pointing to me and gesturing towards the field. I stared at them motionless, gripping my glass of beer. Watched them walk back together to our table. My friend leaned down, grinned at me and said, 'Come on, let's go'.

We walked down the pavilion steps towards the edge of the turf accompanied by the official; a dream came true. The last (and only) time I had been this close to those steps was when I had sat a stone's throw away, the mind completely scrambled, watching in awe as Clive Lloyd loped down like a panther, the bat a mere toothpick in his gangly arms. And here we were, strolling down casually towards the field, leaving our beers behind on the table. The legs were suddenly heavy, laden with the weight of history.

The walk out to the middle was chilling.

Did I crane my neck and squint at the dark sky as I had seen many of my heroes do to adjust their eyes to the light as they crossed the ropes? Perhaps. Treading the very path which generations of cricketers, legends and deified royalty of the game had taken to reach the middle was a hair-raising experience in the moonlight. The stadium expanded in size as we got closer to the middle. The stands receded into the horizon at the same time as they reached towards the sky. I felt our bodies shrinking. Soon we would be hidden in the blades of wet grass we stood on.

The pavilion lights blinked in the distance and the stadium spun around dizzily. I tried to focus my eyes on specific locations in the stands. On the lower deck next to the BEML stand. Upper tier at extra-cover facing the bowling from the pavilion end. Lower deck at square leg from the other end. Searching for the kid, then the teenager and the gangly young man who even shaved. Searching, so that I could reverse that intense gaze and revisit where I sat in those days. Make eye contact, looking intently at the very spot I now stood on.

As I stood that night at the top of the pitch looking towards the sightscreen at the pavilion end, one image glowed in my mind. And I distinctly remember squinting my eyes, imagining the short and stocky figure crouched in that compact stance, eyes in the shadow of that India cap sitting snug on the shock of dark hair, bat tapping methodically as he awaited Andy Roberts running in from far, far yonder...from Antigua itself. And then letting the fizzing delivery pass a foot past his off-stump before he—almost courteously—angled his bat and sent it rocketing to the backward-point boundary.

Straight at where I was sitting that wondrous morning.

The KSCA stadium had materialised magically—almost overnight—in my life. Growing up in south Bangalore, the part of the city it is located in was almost an alternate universe to us back then. Mahatma Gandhi Road only played cameo roles in a child's mind—Brigade Road, Christmas lights and store window Santas knee-deep in white cotton snow. Visits to movie theatres like Lido, Rex, Plaza and Galaxy—the magical screens that shimmered with epic movies like *The Sound of Music*, *Chitty Chitty Bang Bang*, *The Guns of Navarone*, *The Day of the Jackal* and *Enter the Dragon*. These visits culminated—most of the time—in mouth-watering ice-cream specials at Lakeview. Aah, the Cassata, the Merry Widow special...

Those were the wondrous days.

Cricket was just budding in the imagination. Devoid of television imagery, it was embroiled in a web of incomplete stories, myths, rants, theories and smorgasbords of opinion inflicted on us by fathers, uncles and grandfathers. You always found them clustered around giant glowing contraptions that served as radios, faces knotted up in concentration, ears cocked at the crackly signals being beamed in from god knows where. Sometimes, things got scary—people snarled, shouted and bared their teeth. These were divided families—divided by the tactics and strategies they espoused and dispensed to the hapless captain, who was fortunate to escape the cacophony. They stood united in their support of the state and national team, but were willing to disown each other in a flash over a bowling change or field placement.

But in Bangalore, there was no risk of familial bonds fracturing amidst the stress of these cricket matches. None whatsoever. For, peace was always lurking around the corner. When fathers, uncles and grandfathers united, faces softened, understanding and reassuring smiles broke out. Their voices turned gentle and conciliatory. Even the mothers and grandmothers looking on exasperatedly at the hordes in front of the radio would sit back and smile affectionately.

For he was at the crease.

He was Viswa before he was Vishy. He will always be Viswa to us who grew up in Bangalore. I don't think I even knew that the 'G' stood for Gundappa back then. I do know for a fact that I knew Viswa before I knew cricket. How could I not? His name was the first word-association I ever made with cricket. He was special before I even realised how special he was. Or why. For we kids saw it in the eyes of everyone at home and all over the city; eyes which glowed with affection above anything else. The affection and fiercely protective sentiment towards him was overpowering. Amongst cities of North India, Kanpur now superseded Delhi in our minds.

He had made it so.

And thus began our cricket education—in the sole pursuit and study of Viswa. Radio commentary was endured as others batted, exasperatingly delaying his arrival at the crease. Fielding positions were memorised and learnt (with diagrams on sheets of paper) by listening to commentators describe his shots around the green. Back alley attempts at 'Viswanath goes down on his knee and drives through the off-side' were a daily ritual. The square cut and the late cut—of course, were put on pedestals. Spectacularly late cuts were attempted, inspired by still photographs. Most of them ended in hit-wicket dismissals. But we were the naïve and the undeterred.

It was during a family trip to Cubbon Park, which abuts the Chinnaswamy Stadium on the one side, that the still under construction arena loomed into view. It appeared massive. Bamboo scaffolding crisscrossed its entirety on the exterior and construction crews were at work on a war footing. To a kid, the structure looked ominous. So, this is how Lord's and Eden Gardens look, we thought amongst ourselves. And we dreamt of feats of magic that awaited there. Dreamt of 'the cover-drive on one knee' and the 'delectable late cut'. They were building it for him to showcase himself to his city, we said to ourselves. And we dreamt of watching him in action there.

I was yet to witness a cricket match in a stadium.

Then came the news that would change everything—the first Test match of the tour of the West Indies in 1974 had been granted to the still half-complete KSCA stadium. A Test match! Against the West Indies! Gary Sobers, Rohan Kanhai and Lance Gibbs were coming, we assumed from our eavesdropping on the relentless chatter going on in our homes. Fast bowlers who made batsmen run for their life were the norm in that team, we were warned. Hadn't one of them almost killed an Indian captain by cracking his skull open? Now they would be playing in our city? Against our Viswa? Gulp!

All of this was magical and seemed almost improbable. Endless evenings were spent discussing and imagining the events of this match in the months that preceded it. Yes, it was like that back then. Matches of this magnitude had epic build-ups of anticipation uncluttered by relentless cricket. But the very thought of being at the stadium to witness the match was so far-fetched that it had never crossed my mind. Till the day my father came home from work and ceremoniously fished out two strips of paper from his briefcase and waved it around my face.

He had two tickets to all five days of the Test match in his hand!

ജ

The footprints of history can be very ruthless with memories. Retrospect and hindsight can skew perceptions and recollections to such an extent that all that is left is a blur. Childhood memories are never microscopes—always kaleidoscopes. My fate was to be doomed as far as this match was concerned—for life. All that and more was to come much later. But 22 November 1974 would be the beginning of a cricket journey and an enchantment that would endure.

Feverish can be the best description of my state on the first day of that match as I jostled through the throngs around the stadium, hanging onto my father's shirt-tails. Just the bus ride up had been an experience. Bishen Bedi had been left out of the team and shouting matches broke out repeatedly between groups of people on the bus over it. And no Kanhai too, they spluttered exasperatedly. I couldn't care less as I looked out of the window dreamily. He was in the team. He would be there when India batted. This was all about him, for me. Would he dazzle us all? Would Clive Lloyd pick him up and cradle him like Tony Greig had done?

Awestruck would be an understatement of my reaction to the first sighting of the expanse of the turf and the stands that day. Even with half the stadium uncovered and the other half sporting a makeshift roof held up by bamboo poles, it looked spectacular to me. And it was packed to the rafters—I had never seen that many people in my life! As the Indian team walked out onto the field led by Tiger Pataudi, my eyes sought out the short and diminutive profile and locked on him all the way to the middle. There he was, in the flesh.

I was finally in the presence of Viswa.

We were made to wait to see him with a bat in his hand, for the Windies batted first. The day was spent watching him flit about the field. He looked so tiny! Meanwhile, Alvin Kallicharan set about the Indian bowling with a dazzling century. It must have been dazzling, for he was being paid the ultimate Bangalore compliment by the admiring spectators that day: 'Bats just like a left-handed Viswa, doesn't he?' they smiled at each other knowingly. And Gordon Greenidge, who stamped himself on the sport, wasting no time whatsoever on his debut.

Our hearts were in our mouths when India came out to bat—when we saw Roberts and Vanburn Holder mark out their bowling run-ups at the foot of the sight screen! It seemed improbable and inhuman. And boy, were they fast! Viswanath's innings that day was lost, shrouded in the mists of time. But what lingers vividly is the nervous energy that rippled through the Bangalore crowd as he came out to bat. As does the moment when he hit a six—probably off Gibbs. And one of his delectable specials, that came thudding into the cover-point fence directly in front of us.

Not yet at an age when I was allowed to walk to school by myself, I was to receive a bonus prize on the third day of the match. My father suddenly acquired an extra ticket—this time in the pavilion! I was dropped off at the entrance with strict instructions about where to meet him at lunch and tea. I had settled down, a stone's throw away from those very pavilion steps. All I can recall from the day's events is watching the players from close proximity as they exited and returned to the dressing rooms looking like otherworldly giants—especially Lloyd. And that scary moment, when my entire section ducked for cover as a bludgeoning hit from his bat came whistling over our heads during his innings, one that can be legitimately certified as a massacre. Even by today's standards.

All that survives of the entirety of that match is a hazy blur. In a child's world of miracles and supermen, every actor on that stage left behind streaks and trails that glow in the imagination. Time may have eroded away the minutiae and visual evidence from the memory bank, but what endures stubbornly is the sheer magic of witnessing a cricket match, a Test match, in a stadium for the first time. The tales of wonder passed on by generations about the feats of magicians like MAK Pataudi, Erapalli Prasanna, Bhagwat Chandrashekar and Sunil Gavaskar now had a basis in reality. And the players of the West Indies—already dangerously exalted in impressionable minds—took on an even more mythological status, a status which would only get reinforced over the coming years.

Aah, yes, there was the small matter of the other debutant for the West Indies in the Test match alongside Gordon Greenidge.

Yes…him…

I had walked into the KSCA Stadium that morning holding onto my father's hand with a laser-focused quest on my mind. I went to find my Viswa—and I would taste sweet victory in that. But I had no inkling that I was about to get blindsided by another man who would strike me like lightning, leave me reeling. A man who would come to embody my very interest in cricket in the years that followed. A man who would put a spell on me and hold my mind in a vice-like grip till the day he retired; a grip, which in fact hasn't loosened a bit to this day. I would remain spellbound by the power of his presence, his aura and his majesty. To this day, I cannot think of him without a smile breaking out on my happy face.

Isaac Vivian Alexander Richards.

Richards set his foot and his first imprint onto the pages of cricket history in Bangalore that day in November—and unbeknownst to me at the time, I surrendered. Capitulated, in fact, to his overpowering presence and magnificence for the next two decades. That regal and aquiline nose, the smouldering eyes under the dark shadow of his maroon cap, the foreboding swagger and the beads of sweat on his muscular forearms are images burnt into my consciousness. Images that never fail to flit across my eyes even now within minutes of watching any cricket—be it live or on television. He was to dazzle and capture my imagination to such an extent with his mesmerising presence that all others who followed were doomed to pale in comparison.

He is the sole reason that I have lost complete objectivity when it comes to my recollections of those fateful five days at the KSCA Stadium in 1974. He barely caused a ripple, other than to draw the ire of cynics in the crowd who held him responsible for Kanhai's absence in the team. Oh, he was to make them rue their cynicism in spades soon, mind you. But my obsession with Richards that followed has coloured and tinted all opinions and memories I have from that match irreparably. And in spite of all the details of that Test match filled in meticulously in the years since, I can no longer vouch any more for the authenticity of my own experience of them. He made his debut and I was there. The aura of the match was now in the stratosphere.

'Love at first sight,' wrote the eminent cricket writer Gideon Haigh about his relationship with the sport. I can aspire to nothing more eloquent and can only co-opt his words in describing my experience of stepping into the confines of the KSCA Stadium that November. The years that followed would gradually morph the awe it had inspired into a cozy and reassuring familiarity. The playground of dreams would become the arena of thrills. And the ensemble that made up its glorious cast would grow richer and more varied—Bishen Bedi, Mohinder Amarnath, Kapil Dev, Dilip Vengsarkar, Malcolm Marshall, Ian Botham, Geoffrey Boycott, David Gower, Zaheer Abbas, Imran Khan, Javed Miandad, Allan Border, Kim Hughes... and on and on.

Yes, memorable were the acts that followed them and epic were their feats in my mind. But no one would ever capture the soul like Viswanath and Richards had.

Viswa and Viv.

They, more than anyone, would be intertwined with the Chinnaswamy Stadium for me. Viswa, who had nurtured and mouth-fed cricket to me. And Viv, who would come to justify every subsequent moment I invested in the sport.

I walked out to the pitch that day and, in a flash, had found myself there. Stumbled over my childhood and the cricketing teeth left there in the middle by the tooth fairy. The earth in the pitch shone in the moonlight and as I peered down, I saw my own wide-eyed reflection in it. And I saw Viswa looming behind one shoulder, smiling shyly back. Saw that dazzling smile on Viv's face towering behind the other.

I was fortunate to be sent out onto the pitch that moonlit night at the Chinnaswamy Stadium as a night watchman. And like any good night watchman, I tried to hold on to one end and the memories that lived there.

Viswa and Viv would take care of the other.

Postscript

Today, its motif and imagery is awash with colour. It even has dancing girls! The erstwhile KSCA lingers as a monochrome doppelganger of the Chinnaswamy.

Time is up to its illusory tricks and the stadium appears to have shrunk in size. But even today, when the players don their whites and the people of Bangalore choose to pack the rafters, it can turn the clock back. The turf glows and the stands once again recede into the distance. The kaleidoscopic view of childhood dreams still radiates from its middle. Bask in it and you can find your own Viswa or Viv to treasure. And cherish.

Sriram Dayanand dabbles in writing about cricket, music and culture from Toronto, Canada. His scribbles have appeared in ESPNCricinfo, *Sports Illustrated India*, *Pop Matters*, *Mint Lounge* and *Yahoo! Cricket*. He is convinced that his promising cricket career was cut short by an inability to know where his off-stump was. Or leg-stump, for that matter.

Gold, Silver and Bronze

KP Mohan

Usha inspired a whole generation of girls, aspiring Olympians, no matter that she failed to grab the Olympic medal by that now-famous hundredth of a second. For a nation perpetually engaged in following the fortunes of the cricketers, if not submerged in political cacophony, she gave something extra to shout about.

'I don't intend coming back to the camp next season,' she said. A matter of fact statement, said without any rancour, but in a tone that suggested she meant business. 'Then, is it your last meet?' I asked, slightly taken aback, for there was no indication earlier in the season that she might be thinking of quitting. 'Don't write it now. The federation people may put pressure,' she said.

How wrong she was!

That was at the Tatya Tope Stadium in Bhopal on 27 October 1999, on the eve of the Open National. The end-season fatigue had gripped almost all the athletes. PT Usha was no exception. As usual, she was being mobbed by everyone around—children, volunteers, officials and policemen.

Amidst the blaring music and the commotion all around on rehearsal day, one managed to exchange a few more words before rushing off to write the day's copy for *The Hindu*. There was the temptation to write that this was going to be the last meet for the greatest athlete India had ever seen. That temptation was resisted and the point buried in the report more as a hint than as a firm statement.

One had the feeling that she would come back once she had sorted out the mental tussle, the agony which every woman, in her post-motherhood comeback, has to go through; of leaving her child back home when getting down to the business of running. 'If you are my mother, then why are you staying away from me for so long?' Seven-year-old Ujjwal had started asking some awkward questions. The athletics icon had no answer. She just shed tears.

One remembered a similar scene, back in Kuala Lumpur in 1991. Tears welled up in Shiny Wilson's eyes, as she finished talking to people at home after her victory in the 400m at the Asian Track and Field (ATF) meet. It was her comeback and she was overjoyed, but her little daughter Shilpa was waiting for her return.

Their careers running almost parallel, Usha and Shiny were the two pillars of Indian women's athletics through the 1980s and 1990s. Usha, of course, towered above everyone else, but she did not have the same success as Shiny on her comeback, at least in clocking timings she might have been aiming for. Shiny had a sub-two for the 800m at Madras in 1995 to realise a long-cherished dream while Usha's goal of a sub-23 for the 200m remained unfulfilled.

Studies have shown—some of the all-time greats have also proved by their own examples—that women do gain in strength and endurance after childbirth, through hormonal changes. But long periods of absence from home make mothers far too vulnerable psychologically than anyone else in the sports field—more so in the

Indian context. There have been outstanding examples of mothers making great comebacks in international athletics. Fanny Blankers-Koen, the Dutch all-rounder, for one; Irena Szewinska, the Polish sprinter for another. German long jumper Heike Drechsler, if one was to take a deviation from the track. Or British marathoner Liz McColgan. But then, the Indian mothers apparently find the task a lot tougher, off the track. Yet, Usha was prepared to give it a last try, her best shot, much to her critics' dismay and her rivals' misery. At least that is what she felt at the beginning of 2000. She thought that her injured left knee would respond to Ayurvedic treatment and, more importantly, she would be wanted.

She was wrong on both counts. Her knee took more time to mend. In fact, it never allowed her to feel completely comfortable. She missed much of her offseason training and the entire first phase of the competition circuit. She seemed to have run out of time; the girl from Payyoli who ran against the clock all the time was at last beaten by it even before the race had started. Still, she talked about coming back in time for the rescheduled All-India Inter-State Meet, even as speculation intensified that the Asian Championships would be postponed to November. Usha's hopes soared all over again.

But the very same Amateur Athletic Federation of India (AAFI), which in the past used to plead with her took her name out of the campers list. She was told to inform the federation in writing about her intentions and her training programme. Only then was it prepared to consider her in its Olympic and Asian calculations.

Usha complied, but felt hurt, to put it mildly. Humiliated would be more appropriate. Natural for someone who had given everything she had to the country, someone who showed the way to a generation of young athletes, someone who was a household name across the length and breadth of the country, someone who could raise the stature of a meet by her mere presence.

'Should I?' became the question. Should I try once more when I am not wanted? The news that the Asian Championships would, after all, come off at the end of August more or less clinched it. In between came the record-shattering streak in Kiev and in Bangalore by KM Beenamol, Rachita Mistry and Vinita Tripathi, which left her clutching a sixteen-year-old national mark in the 400m hurdles and little else. Usha stirred up a controversy as well as a meaningful debate by demanding that the record-breakers be tested. Deep inside her she had this fear of losing out to opponents who might not have been 'clean' in her own assessment. Having been part of the national camps through 1998 and 1999, the phase in which the doping virus had hit Indian athletics in the most decisive manner, Usha knew a lot more than those of us crying foul from the other side of the fence. One had probed her mind through the previous months about her continuation and what she had in store. Thus, when she rang up on the night of July 24 and brought up the subject of retirement from international athletics towards the end of that conversation, there never was any great surprise.

'Do you want to announce it in Delhi or back home?' I asked. Next morning, she settled for the Kerala House in New Delhi. The last time, too, it was in New Delhi, at the Nehru Stadium, immediately on return from the Beijing Asian Games in 1990. Ten years had passed and Usha had survived; survived despite the back-biting, the injuries, setbacks and losses. She had the perseverance, that blinkered approach and a confidence in her ability which separates the greats from the good ones. Emotionally, however, she had always been susceptible. Usha could get upset at the slightest of provocations. She was distraught when columnists wrote that she was shamming prior to the 1988 Olympics. 'Shamming for what? To avoid whom? I wasn't the Olympic champion to avoid someone,' Usha said years ago.

'People who write such crap should get themselves injected with cortisone under their heels,' said Dr (Major) PSM Chandran, of the Sports Authority of India (SAI) those days. That was what Usha was getting: cortisone injections under her painful heel. Usha crashed out in the heat of the Olympic 400m hurdles and was excluded from the longer relay team after a farcical trial (she ran alone) was gone through in Seoul. A decade hence, at Bangkok, no trial was held but the situation was more or less similar. Usha was eventually left out, leaving her in tears. She was certain that, injury or not, she was capable of running better than the fourth runner, Jincy Philip. She wept in Lucknow in 1994 when she was asked to run all alone in the 200m as a trial for the Hiroshima Asian Games. She was insulted again at the 1995 South Asian Federation (SAF) Games in Madras (now Chennai) when the national flag was snatched away from her before the closing ceremony began. She was the captain and she was told that she would be carrying the flag. Despite her emotional fragility, Usha showed tremendous mental strength in continuing with a career that had not really taken off on her comeback in 1993. For her, the aim was to better her own marks. On the way, if the medals came, it was great. 'She is power-running nowadays,' commented the former national coach JS Saini as one discussed her cramped style and lack of smoothness in her arm and knee action in a meet in Delhi prior to the 1994 Asian Games.

To her credit, she clocked close to her personal best in 1997 and 1998, equalled her 200m national record of 23.27s twice at Fukuoka, Japan, in the 1998 Asian Meet and then met with a huge setback at the Calcutta Inter-State close to the Bangkok Asiad. A hamstring had popped and her well-chalked-out plans for the Asian Games had gone completely awry even before she set foot in the Thai capital. Hope springs eternally and Usha was not without that precious commodity at Bangkok. But the missed training sessions, the lack of race fitness and her age worked against her. Plus of course a set of teammates, all junior to her, who seemed to have left their manners and sporting spirit back home.

It was a surprise that Usha chose to pursue her career after the Bangkok debacle. 'Whatever I wanted to achieve, I couldn't do it in Bangkok. I had to satisfy myself that I was capable of reaching those goals,' said Usha in defence of her decision to continue.

The camps were her problem, the days spent away from home and family. Obviously, she could not have depended solely on her own training on the beaches of Payyoli. From the Payyoli beaches through the grind of school meets, district meets and national meets to the global arena of the Olympic Games, then through the 1982 Asian Games, several ATF meets and an umpteen number of other internationals, it had been a stirring saga of fortitude and sacrifices of resilience and a single-minded pursuit of excellence. In OM Nambiar, she had a coach who could drive her towards her goals. A rather abrasive man, who protected and treated her like his daughter. Many 'experts' had commented that Usha would have been better off had she trained for a year or more in the US after the Los Angeles Olympics. 'I got only offers of physical education scholarships,' she clarified at her press conference in New Delhi. Usha was never the outgoing type. She needed Nambiar for everything. Perhaps her mental make-up was not suited for a prolonged period of stay abroad, all alone.

Many have also pointed out that had she run in a series of top-level competitions abroad before going to the Los Angeles Olympics, the story might have been different, history could have been made. She could only go where she was entered by the federation. She was not a professional athlete who could negotiate with promoters, agents and meet organisers. Los Angeles proved her most memorable achievement as well as the most disappointing moment in a glittering career, going by her own words. Perhaps the 1986 Seoul Asian Games will vie for the second slot, if not an equal place, though Nambiar rates the 1985 Jakarta ATF feat of five gold medals as her best. In the post-1988 Olympics phase, when she suffered her first defeat at home, by Ashwini Nachappa, only to sweep her rivals and critics out of sight with a stand-out show in New Delhi in the 1989 ATF, Usha showed a willingness to take on punishing loads.

Nambiar was a great motivator, not to speak of the tough taskmaster that he always was. But Beijing 1990 had something else in store. Against a well-prepared Chinese team, Usha was left licking her wounds, fourth in the 200m and second in the 400m behind Li Guilian, despite clocking a 52.86. Still, retirement looked a hasty decision. Marriage to V Sreenivasan, a kabaddi player from the Police, in 1991, and the arrival of Ujjwal in 1992, slowly helped Usha put her Beijing memories behind and shift her focus back to the track. The comeback was made in 1993, though without competing in any of the major meets. Her Hiroshima voyage next year was uneventful, but she enjoyed the attention she received all the same. There will never be any unanimity of views about her comeback. Many have argued that it was the most foolish decision an athlete of Usha's stature could have taken; many others point out the excellent results, close to her all-time bests plus a national record she had, from 1997 to 1999, as justification enough for her return to the track. And she contributed handsomely to the short relay gold and the silver in the longer relay at the Fukuoka Asian meet, apart from winning two individual bronze medals. Usha only partially achieved what she had set out to. She would have surely wanted an individual gold at the Asian level on her return. That was not to be. She would have also wanted a sub-23 for the 200m and an improvement on her 51.61s for the one-lapper. That also was not to be. Yet, when she finally settles down on the pages of Indian athletics history, she can proudly say that she tried hard to achieve her goals till the age of thirty-six. How many of us can say that?

Usha inspired a whole generation of girls, aspiring Olympians, no matter that she failed to grab the Olympic medal by that now-famous hundredth of a second. For a nation perpetually engaged in following the fortunes of the cricketers, if not submerged in the political cacophony, she gave something extra to shout about.

Her exploits were discussed around the world and at home; successive governments, both at the centre and in her state, vied with each other to encourage her. Many rate her as the greatest Indian sportsperson of the past century, though she remains the humble girl from Payyoli, the little town in Kerala. Oh, yes, she has grown, is a mother and can handle a lot many things on her own. Finally, the time had come to say goodbye. Back home, Ujjwal should be happy. But then, the little fella better watch out. The Usha School of Athletics is on the anvil, and his mother might turn her full attention towards yet another dream of hers. For Usha, dreams never die; they are an unending medley.

Postscript

Almost a dozen years on, Usha still has her dreams going uninterrupted. The Usha School of Athletics, near Kozhikode, has become a nursery for budding talent in Kerala. Among them is 800m runner Tintu Luka on whom Usha has great hopes for the future.

Usha slogs it out for her school just as she used to slog in her preparations for big championships. Ujjwal, now into his second year in an MBBS course, does not complain about not receiving that much attention.

Though she has matured beyond her running days, Usha still is a highly emotional person and can easily get upset over little things. 'Sometimes I feel all these efforts of running an athletics school are a waste. People try to discourage you, criticise you, find fault with almost everything,' Usha said in a recent conversation.

But she has had support, from public and private entities. Even as she values such support, Usha continues to be fiercely independent and proud. Her goal is an Olympic medal. She is grooming Luka for the next Olympics, and waiting in the wings is another middle distance prodigy, Jessy Joseph.

KP Mohan has been writing on athletics for more than thirty years. Since 1991 he has covered several international athletics championships including the World Championships and the Asian Championships. He has followed the career of PT Usha since she was sixteen. Apart from athletics and multi-discipline games his interests include doping in sports. He is currently based in New Delhi as a Deputy Editor with *The Hindu*.

Oh! The Premature Epitaph

Sandeep Nakai

[Before the Netherlands went forth to retain the Olympic Games hockey gold, the assertion of player-power had come to the fore in what was to be ascribed as the team sacking the coach. 'We sacked the coach and went on to win the Olympic gold,' was almost the underlying theme of the Dutch team.]

Frustration, anger, disgust...the atmosphere in the Netherlands locker-room was fraught with escalating rage after the team that claimed to play faultless hockey faltered in their last round-robin league outing of the 2000 Olympic Games against Pakistan.

Fancied to become the first team to win back-to-back Olympic gold medals since India's glorious run of six successive titles ended in 1956, the Netherlands had arrived at Sydney with a most formidable reputation as title holders in the Olympics, World Cup and Champions Trophy—hockey's version of a Grand Slam.

Not everything, however, was well between the team management, which was personified by the coach, and the players, in whose ranks were several seasoned players that included Olympic and World Cup gold medallists. This was a special generation of Dutch players, who had broken away from the defence-oriented stereotype to showcase their dazzling skills, thereby altering the complexion of world hockey forever.

The Stephan Veen-led Dutch team did not always follow the coach's line; and coach Maurits Hendriks was adamant that he knew the strategies best. Hendriks had been the deputy in the coaching hierarchy during the successful campaigns of the 1996 Atlanta Olympics and the 1998 World Cup, and took over from chief coach Roelant Oltmans, who retired after the World Cup triumph in front of an admiring home audience at Utrecht.

The Dutch team was packed with ten gold medallists from the champion side of the last Olympics, and several more from the World Cup when Hendriks took charge of the squad with one-and-a-half-year to go for the Sydney Olympics.

Brimming with experienced players, the Dutch believed that they knew the skills of the trade well enough. The simmering tension was just beneath the surface, even though this heady combination had earlier won the Champions Trophy at Amstelveen that summer to reinforce their status as the favourites for the Olympic title.

Things were falling into place as the Netherlands stayed atop the Group A table with one round-robin league match to go. Two wins and two draws in four games had the Dutch team in the group table's leading slot, based on their marginal edge in goal-difference over Germany, who too had an equal number of points. Pakistan had not beaten the Netherlands in the past seven encounters and the defending champions played true to form to enjoy overwhelming domination in this encounter as well. But goals proved elusive, despite the Dutch strikers having as many as fourteen shots at the Pakistan goal and forcing nine penalty corners. Playing an outstanding game,

Pakistan goalkeeper Ahmed Alam stood like a rock between the Netherlands strikers and the citadel.

At the other end, drag-flick specialist Sohail Abbas put three-time Olympic gold medallists Pakistan ahead in the twentieth minute. Kashif Javed put the game beyond the Dutch team's reach on Pakistan's fourth and final penalty corner in the sixty-seventh minute when he captalised on a rebound from goalkeeper Ronald Jansen's pads.

The Dutch dream was all but shattered by this 0-2 loss to Pakistan, who had managed to thwart a wave of raids to secure a semifinal berth.

Elimination at the preliminary pool stage was on the anvil when the Dutch stepped off the turf with their shoulders stooping, their hopes almost in tatters when European hockey rivals Germany and Britain stepped on to the pitch for the last pool match. A draw would be enough to secure former champions Germany a spot in the semi-final at the expense of the Netherlands.

Germany, however, were out to seal the issue with an emphatic victory, what with their opponents for the last round-robin league, Britain, lying at the bottom of the pool standings without a single win in four previous outings. With two points through two drawn encounters, Britain were among the under-achievers of this competition.

The painful realisation of their winning spree coming to an end was compounded by a locker room flare-up which saw matters come to a boil on that September evening at Homebush Bay. Just as the Germany-Britain game was getting underway, Dutch coach Hendriks was pronouncing his team dead and gone, and the epitaph came with a verbal lashing.

The players, dejected at the loss and furious at the coach's comments, emerged from that post-match conclave distraught.

From what they absorbed and understood, the terse message said it was the players and their ill-conceived ideas about game-strategy that had resulted in the loss. The defeat was attributed to the players' obstinate behaviour and inability to execute the game-plan, which indicated a failure on the part of the players, and not the coach.

But that was not the end of the Netherlands story at the Sydney Olympics. There was another twist in the fate that brought the Dutch back into the fray and spiked the soaring German ambitions. If the robust German team was expecting a stroll into the semifinals after the Dutch slump, it was dashed by a resurgent outfit from Britain, which finally produced a fine match after an indifferent tournament.

Following a goalless first half in which Britain matched the pace of their formidable rivals, German captain Christian Mayerhoffer opened the scoring with a field goal two minutes into the second session. Britian equalised four minutes later on a penalty corner conversion by Craig Parnham. A draw would still be enough to take the Germans ahead of the Dutch, and they were quite aware of that. Still comfortably ensconced with scores level and just five minutes to go for the hooter, the Germans got a rude jolt, on a cold and breezy day, when a penalty corner essay from Calum Giles brooked no denial. His shot soared over custodian Christopher Reitz to turn the form-book upside down, leaving the Germans dazed. There was no further drama even as the Germans went all out for an equaliser, for the British defenders held their ground to pull off a shock win.

Out of the blue, the Netherlands were back from the dead and had sneaked into the semifinals on the basis of their slight edge in goal difference, despite being level with Germany on eight points from five outings. The Netherlands had a superior goal difference with eleven goals for and eight against, compared to Germany's seven for and six against. Three days later, when Germany came face-to-face with Britain again in the playoffs for the fifth position, the Germans fired four goals without reply, but it was no consolation for the earlier lapse that deprived them of a chance to claim a medal.

The sequence of crazy results of that day continued as Poland later breached the Indian defence for an equaliser in the penultimate minute to break the hearts of a billion people. India seemed on course for a semifinal two decades after winning the last of their eight gold medals in the boycott-hit Moscow Olympics in 1980, only to squander their chances, but that is another story. South Korea and India were tied on points and had an identical goal difference behind group toppers Australia. The tie was resolved by the result of the pool encounter between these two teams that the Koreans had won.

Thereafter it was veteran goalkeeper Ronald Jansen, making his farewell appearance in international sport, who was called to action in successive penalty shootouts in the semifinals against hosts Australia and then the title encounter against surprise finalists South Korea. It was then time for Jansen to dive across and block the penalty flicks after his ear-splitting instructions to defenders had performed their task during regulation period and extra-time of the crux encounters, on which depended whether the Dutch roller-coaster ride continued for the second successive Olympic Games.

When Jansen twice emerged from the penalty shootouts throwing celebratory punches in the air, the Netherlands had achieved the incredible. Jansen's third Olympic Games appearance, sixteen years after he first emerged with a bronze medal in Seoul, was the culmination of an illustrious journey etching his name in the annals of Dutch hockey.

With Jansen in the goal, the Netherlands backed themselves to win the tie-breaker every time, but the scenario was not always quite as rosy. In fact, the Dutch had over the years been feeling the pangs of frustration in penalty shootouts and had to bring in sports psychologists to work with the players.

The penalty shootout loss in the final of the 1994 World Cup in Sydney, which was followed by a similar defeat to Germany in the European Cup, still rankled, but it was no longer at the back of the Dutch players' mines when they stepped up to take the penalty flicks in these Olympics.

To English psychologist John Syer went the credit for shaping the Netherlands into deadly penalty-stroke executioners, and the team management contributed by training seven players to take the flicks. Goalkeeper Jansen, of course, was not among those who needed help from sports psychologists. The joke often cited in Dutch hockey circles was that sports psychologists ought to have been sent to Jansen for training.

A successful businessman and a star player in his own reckoning, Jansen for a time did not feature in the Netherlands squad because he refused to take second position behind Frank Leistra, and had caused some commotion when he played without face protection during the 1987 European Nations Cup at Amstelveen. His steely nerves were called into play in crunch tie-breaker situations twice in the space of three days, setting the stage for him to cap his career by featuring in two penalty shootout victories.

Custodian Jansen brought off two outstanding saves during the first half of the semifinals, which were the closest the Australian strikers got to the Dutch goal. The encounter remained goalless after regulation and extra time despite both teams exhibiting attacking hockey, needing a tie-breaker to decide the finalist.

The penalty shootout, too, was decided on the last stroke, taken by Australian Brent Livermore, who came in after all previous strokes had been converted from both teams. Bram Lomans, Wouter van Pelt, Piet-Hein Geeris, captain Veen and Marten Eikelboom had scored for the Netherlands, while Michael Brennan, Troy Elder, Adam Commens and James Elmer had shot on target for Australia. The Netherlands led 5-4 before the final flick that was pushed wide by Livermore, and hosts Australia's hopes of an Olympic hockey gold medal evaporated yet again.

The Netherlands moved into an unfamiliar Olympic final opponent in South Korea, who rode on a fifty-seventh-minute penalty corner conversion by Song Seung-Tae to spike Pakistan's challenge in the semifinal.

The South Korean men, who rose to reckoning in the international hockey scenario when they won the 1986 Asian Games gold medal at Seoul, adopted Japanese 'Kamikaze' tactics to blunt Pakistan's crack penalty corner shooter Sohail Abbas. Deciding not to allow any space for Abbas to execute his rasping drag-flicks, the Koreans had worked out a dangerous plan to run straight at him from the goal-line.

Aware of the injury threat associated with the plan, Korean coach Kim Sang-Ryul was prepared to pay the price and had prepared four players to go for it one after the other. The impact of this suicidal tactic, which denied Abbas a goal for the first match in these Olympic Games, was felt by Korean defender Lim Jung-Woo. Lim was carried off on a stretcher after being struck above the knee and missed playing the final.

Having negated Pakistan's edge in six penalty corners, it was the South Koreans who capitalised on a set-piece variation to storm into the gold medal match.

The aftermath of the coach writing the premature epitaph continued to create a flutter within the Dutch camp. Matters had come to a boil, provoking the players to assert that the coach step aside and they would play their own game. A clear message had gone across: victory or defeat hereafter would be of the players alone. It was not quite the ideal setting for a tactically fine-tuned team going into the business end of the Olympic hockey competition, but the experienced Dutch team had spoken its mind.

The Netherlands enjoyed territorial domination in the final, which was an apt exhibition of modern hockey tactics perfected to an art form. Brisk, speedy counter-attacks using the width of the pitch entertained the spectators and defenders on either end showed their adeptness in falling back and narrowing the gaps.

It was South Korea who opened the scoring through ace striker Song Seung-Tae, who was quick to pick up a rebound and shoot home in the ninth minute. The Netherlands drew parity in the twentieth minute through a deft penalty stroke by skipper Veen after a penalty corner shot from Bram Lomans was blocked on the goal-line by defender Jeon Jong-Ha with his body. Veen went on to score a hat-trick in regulation period and made no mistake with his penalty stroke when the match again went to the tie-breaker.

Two minutes into the second half, the Dutch striking machine pierced open the Korean defence and paved the way for Veen to apply the finishing touches to a move shaped by Marten Eikelboom and Tuen de Nooijer. With just six minutes to go and the Koreans pushing hard in search of an equaliser, Veen completed his hat-trick as he picked up a stray ball and went past two defenders before slotting the ball into the goal.

The Dutch seemed to have done enough to claim the gold medal again, but for the Korean tenacity. Throwing everything into the attack, the nippy Koreans scored twice in the last four minutes of play and tied the scores 3-3 at the end of regulation period.

The Koreans earned their first penalty corner of the match in the sixty-sixth minute and Kim Kyung-Seok began the rally by shooting home on a rebound after goalkeeper Jansen had blocked the shot from captain Kang Keo-Wook.

The Koreans kept up the pressure and were rewarded with another penalty corner two minutes later. Even though the ball was not stopped properly, some brisk thinking saw them relay a pass to Kang, whose brilliant deflection ended in the net and the Asian challengers were back in the hunt.

The Olympic Games hockey arena had never witnessed such a dramatic recovery, and the contest again went to the tie-breaker as extra-time failed to produce a goal, despite both teams playing attacking hockey in search of a gold-clinching goal.

The Netherlands won their second successive penalty shootout 5-4, with Song Seung-Tae being the lone player muffing his flick. The Dutch, expectedly, converted all their penalty strokes with Lomans, Geeris, van Pelt, Eikelboom and Veen landing on target from the spot. Jeon Jong-Ha, Yeo Woon-Kon, Kim Kyung-Seok and captain Kang Keon-Wook scored for South Korea, but Song faltered. South Korea had to be content with the silver medal, but they had achieved the Korean men's biggest prize so far.

Before the Netherlands went forth to retain the Olympic Games hockey gold, the assertion of player-power had come to the fore in what was to be ascribed as the team sacking the coach. 'We sacked the coach and went on to win the Olympic gold,' was almost the underlying theme of the Dutch team in the final, which was the swansong for skipper Veen.

Veen seemed to have reserved his best for the last, cornering the spotlight through his dazzling goals in open field play. He felt the Dutch players were steeled for the challenge faced in the crunch games after going through an intensely tough period.

'The Dutch again proved what a closely knit team could achieve,' said Veen, an obvious reference to the continuing rift. 'Making the final was like living a dream. After losing to Pakistan, we were quite lost. We wanted to end the competition with a good performance, but I never thought it would be the final.'

Even as the Dutch players celebrated the rare feat of retaining the Olympic hockey gold medal, coach Hendriks stood on the sidelines contemplating his future.

'It's incredible...two golds in a row, you won't see it again soon,' said Hendriks. 'We're talking about a special generation of players.'

The assertion of player-power by this talented generation of Dutch hockey stars meant Hendriks had to alter the course of his coaching assignment, leaving the Netherlands national team after returning home.

Hockey had seen the emergence of player-power like never before. The premature epitaph brought the controversy out of the closet.

Postscript

Maurits Hendriks had to resign as coach of the Netherlands team after the Olympics, but moved to mentor the Spanish national men's team which under his charge, shaped into a strong outfit. During his stint as coach, Spain won the 2004 Champions Trophy and the 2005 European Cup.

Several top stars from this special generation of Dutch players retired after the 2000 Olympics, they still fielded a team that made the final of the Olympic Games in 2004 at Athens where Australia won the men's gold medal for the first time. Player-power asserted itself in various ways across the world, but hockey has not again witnessed such a breakdown between the coach and the players.

Sandeep Nakai, a New Delhi-based sports journalist, has written on hockey for nearly three decades. He has reported on three Olympic Games and six World Cups, beside multiple Asian Games and Commonwealth Games. He is the chairperson of the International Sports Press Association (AIPS) Hockey Commission.

Worth Living for

Anand Philar

'Ok, we checked you out. Please excuse me but you are the first Indian newspaper journalist seeking accreditation, and so it took us a while. I am happy to tell you that we will grant you a Media accreditation. Welcome to Formula One!' she said with a bright smile.

I am not much into miracles, though one did happen that remains vivid in my memory despite the passage of time—well over a decade, to be precise. The incident opened the doors to the glamorous world of Formula One.

Back in 1999, when Formula One was in the process of getting embedded in the Indian psyche, a chance opportunity took me to Kuala Lumpur and thence to the spanking new Sepang International Circuit.

If there is one country other than India where I feel at home, it is Malaysia, which I had first visited in 1980 on a badminton assignment in the wake of Prakash Padukone's exploits. Since then,

I have been a frequent visitor to Kuala Lumpur and seen it grow from a virtual one-street town into a bustling metropolis.

Still, I was not quite prepared when I landed in Kuala Lumpur ahead of its inaugural Formula One Grand Prix. The brand new airport took my breath away when I arrived on a Thursday before the race weekend. The arrival lounge was plastered with Formula One posters with Michael Schumacher prominently figuring in most and it set the mood for a memorable four days.

There were hospitality desks to help Formula One visitors, who were advised to take the train into the city centre for it was cheaper, faster and safer than taxi. The metro line was built for the Commonwealth Games Kuala Lumpur hosted in 1998.

'Formula One?' queried the immigration officer with a knowing smile. 'Enjoy your stay,' he said as he stamped the entry permit in my passport and I was off like a shot to collect my baggage before heading into town.

As I walked out of the Kuala Lumpur Central Station, it was as if the F1 virus had struck the city. Fans wearing their favourite team colours thronged the streets and it being late evening, the lights and music emanating from various pubs were like a shot of adrenaline.

Friday morning I was up early and, along with a friend, drove to the circuit to watch the free practice sessions. As we approached the track, my heartbeat was close to matching the top-end revs of a Formula One car. Parking the vehicle, we made our way towards the underpass and then it hit me.

Even today, the hair stands on end like it did on that Friday when I saw Eddie Irvine flashing over me in his screaming Ferrari. The sound of the V8 engine working flat out was music to my ears and I just couldn't wait to get into the Paddock.

Barely a fortnight earlier, Kuala Lumpur had not been on my radar until I received a Bridgestone Paddock pass through a friend of mine who urged me to join him on the trip. Those days, in *The New Indian Express* where I was heading the sports desk, Formula One coverage was limited to a few paragraphs, but I defied my editor to give it a better spread along with domestic motorsports events.

So, being deep into motorsports, I readily agreed to my friend's offer, though the editor was not easily convinced that we should be giving a 'Malaysian race' so much prominence, especially with no Indian interest.

What I didn't tell him was that I had no Media accreditation, but then, I prayed some 'miracle' would happen that would give me access to the drivers and teams for a series of stories I promised my editor I would be doing.

Thus, I made my way through the turnstiles at the Sepang circuit using the magnetised Paddock card with some trepidation, as the enormity of the assignment engulfed me. Walking down the Paddock lane situated behind the team garages, I gawked at the various plush hospitality tents, mostly populated by journalists on a junket.

I gawked at some of the prettiest women and handsome hunks who, like me, were wandering about the Paddock. I did peek into a couple of the hospitality tents and they literally smelt money, with some of the choicest liquor and wines being served to the privileged.

Of course, the Paddock was far more populated on Sunday when celebrities from various walks of life graced the circuit, lending the occasion a touch of class and glamour.

I soaked in the atmosphere with my nose twitching, not just for a story but also due to the smells of rubber and exhaust fumes. After wandering up and down the Paddock and taking in the sights, I followed sign boards towards the Media Centre, hoping to 'somehow' gain an entry and an accreditation thereafter.

I eventually landed at the foot of the staircase leading to the Media Centre located above the pit lane garages. A turnstile blocked my entry and there was no security guard stationed at that point. I surreptitiously looked around while trying to figure out how I could get past the gate. It was then that the first part of the 'miracle' happened.

I swiped the Paddock pass card at the turnstile and, voila, the gate swung open! I could hardly believe my luck and after a brief hesitation, zipped up the staircase and into the Media Centre. My joy knew no bounds, for I had 'made it'.

However, I was soon brought down to earth as I was accosted by a stern-looking official with a bunch of cards around her neck. 'Excuse me sir, but you are not permitted here. You do not have a Media badge,' she said. 'How did you get in here in the first place?'

I put on my most pained expression and said: 'Is it so? Sorry, I didn't know, but the turnstile opened when I swiped this card.' She pointed to my card and informed me that I was allowed entry only to the Paddock, but not the Media Centre or the pit lane, that was accessible only to accredited journalists.

'Listen, I have come all the way from India to cover this race. I was not aware of the formalities to secure Media accreditation. So, can you please help me get one? If you can't, then I will go straight to the airport from here and take the first flight home. I am a full-time newspaper journalist and I have written a few articles on Formula One,' I told her and handed my visiting card.

She asked me to be seated and disappeared into the media manager's cabin. I was offered coffee and snacks by a Media Centre staff. It was an agonising wait and with each passing minute, I was losing hope.

The second part of the 'miracle' then happened. The lady came out with a smile and invited me into the media manager's cabin.

'Ok, we checked you out. Please excuse me but you are the first Indian newspaper journalist seeking accreditation and so it took us a while. I am happy to tell you that we will grant you a Media accreditation. Welcome to Formula One!' she said with a bright smile.

I filled up a form, submitted a photograph and within minutes I had another access card around my neck. Soon, the staff handed me a bulky Media kit, showed me around the massive work room. 'You can select any seat you want,' an accompanying staff told me. I picked my seat facing a TV monitor. 'Your Media card gives you access to the pit lane also,' she said. 'You can also use the desktop computer to file your reports, sir.'

The Media Centre, like all else in Formula One, functioned with the comforting purr of a Rolls Royce Silver Ghost. Every need of the journalist was met with a smile and, more importantly, with a promptness that reflected super-efficiency.

So much so that I rated the Media Centre a notch higher than what is made available even at the Olympic Games. Data and information flowed copiously, especially during the race as we were flooded with releases on every single incident, big or small, with quotes from the drivers.

Suitably impressed with the facilities, I could hardly believe my luck and immediately got down to work. After familiarising myself with the Media Centre, I walked out to the Paddock, looking for a story. The first person I came across was Sir Jackie Stewart himself, complete with a tweed jacket and a golf cap.

He patiently replied to my queries and asked me about Chennai, that he had visited in 1987 to lay the foundation stone for India's first ever race track. 'I didn't know that there was such a big following for Formula One in India,' he remarked.

I next bumped into David Coulthard. 'Sorry, I am going for a de-brief, but we can meet later,' he said before hurrying off. Disappointed,

I scouted for another 'prey', especially Michael Schumacher who was coming off an injury that he had sustained at the British Grand Prix, where he broke his leg in a high-speed crash.

As such, there was considerable hype around the inaugural Malaysian Grand Prix, with Michael returning to racing after an enforced break to resume his battle with Mika Hakkinen, who was to go on to win the second of his two back-to-back titles in 1999.

I finally did meet Michael, but it was at the routine Media session near the pit lane where the drivers moved in a circle spending a few minutes with each journalist. You barely get to throw a question in view of the crush of reporters and I managed to ask him about his return to the track after the Silverstone accident. He said he was hopeful of a podium finish and he did precisely that.

The Formula One scene those days was tainted with considerable acrimony, with Ferrari at the very centre of most 'off-track action' as critics repeatedly questioned the legality of the cars rolling out of the Maranello factory. It was no different at Sepang and the atmosphere was crackling with tension and suspicion.

While the attention was mostly on the Ferrari and McLaren teams, I chanced upon young Ralf Schumacher who sat alone and was seemingly contemplating his rather disappointing run in Formula One. Having moved to Williams that season, he was apparently unhappy with the outdated Supertec engine.

In fact Ralf, then only twenty-four, was being hailed as a future star, an expectation, as it transpired, he failed to live up to. He spoke at length about his hopes and aspirations and especially living in the shadow of big brother Michael. To my surprise, he was rather forthcoming and it appeared as though I had caught him at the right moment.

Going into that race, Irvine and Hakkinen were jostling for the championship. With Michael out of the frame for the honours, his role was clearly defined and that was to help Irvine win by any means. Michael chose to block the McLaren of Hakkinen and even though he was quicker than his teammate, he allowed Irvine to twice pass him and eventually win the race while himself finishing second.

The Ferrari 1-2 finish meant Irvine taking a four-point lead over Hakkinen with one race, in Japan, remaining. But the story was far from finished. During the post-race scrutiny, the two Ferrari cars were found to have breached technical regulations and the stewards excluded both Irvine and Michael.

By the time the stewards made their decision late that evening, Irvine was winging his way to Hong Kong for a celebratory party. His classic reaction was: 'I was there to win the race which I did and the matter ends there.' Subsequently, Ferrari successfully appealed the decision and both Irvine and Schumacher were reinstated.

It was another matter that Hakkinen drove a brilliant race to win in Japan and clinch the championship while Ferrari clinched the constructors title.

The Sepang race had the crowd on its feet and I remember standing on the Media Centre balcony that was directly over the Ferrari garage. It gave me a fantastic view of the pit stops that lasted less than ten seconds during which the tyres were changed and the car refuelled.

The experience was nerve-tingling and provided a firsthand view of the clockwork precision with which Formula One teams operated. In fact, the slickness with which the teams operated, they were the last word in efficiency.

More than the race, the pit lane walkabout on Saturday was an eye-opener. Walking into the Ferrari garage and watching Michael at close quarters as he discussed set-up with his engineers was an unforgettable experience.

In fact, the Ferrari mechanics even agreed to my request to be allowed to look into the cockpit from close quarters. 'Feel free and take pictures if you wish to,' said one of them. Of course, Michael was out of bounds for me as he was in deep conversation with his engineers and would not like to be disturbed.

Walking down the pit lane, one could notice that the number of mechanics decreased gradually, reflecting the financial muscle of a team. At the time, there was no cap on team spends. The big teams such as Ferrari and McLaren had virtually unlimited budgets for development and testing.

The joke then was that the annual budget of a back-of-the-grid team like Jordan was equivalent to the hamburger spends of Ferrari!

Besides the race, for me the lasting impression of the assignment was the city of Kuala Lumpur that was decked up like a bride for a week. It was fun and frolic time as the city reverberated with parties, literally from dusk to dawn.

The pubs on the streets near China Town, for instance, were 'adopted' by some of the Formula One teams. They were decorated in the particular team colours with the waitresses wearing matching team uniforms.

Bangsar, the popular tourist hangout, was probably the hottest area that also captured the Formula One atmosphere in all its glory. The narrow street lined on either side by pubs, karaoke bars and restaurants was overflowing with crowds, with a live band playing smack in the middle of the road where a stage was built, complete with psychedelic lights.

Mixing with the massive throng were the members of various Formula One teams, enjoying a night out on town, no-holds-barred. The landmark Finnegan's pub with its Irish décor and music was among the more popular spots.

I did get lucky to meet and spend some time with several English-speaking team mechanics, but it was hardly the occasion to chat up on Formula One. 'No shop talk please, it's party time!' pleaded one of them when I persisted with questions on car preparations and, of course, the drivers. 'We work through the year and with all the travelling, there is little time for anything else, and when we get a chance like this, we would like to forget our work,' he said.

Some of the bigger teams leveraged the occasion with promotional activities during which the drivers obliged autograph hunters and also readily posed for photographs with the fans. Obviously, the Ferrari and McLaren events attracted the biggest crowds and it was all but impossible to get an entry into the venues, much less meet the drivers.

I remember the Ferrari party to which supermodels from all over the world were invited and who also attended the Federation Internationale de Automobile (FIA) dinner. The tickets for these exclusive events were in greater demand than those for the race itself. It is my eternal regret that I couldn't attend either of these two parties, pre-occupied as I was with deadlines.

My requests for one-on-one interviews didn't bear fruit. I was told to make a formal approach to the team's communications manager who would then give an appointment after consulting the driver's schedule. It could mean a wait of over a month and more, I was told.

The 1999 Grand Prix set a trend, if not tradition, in Kuala Lumpur that over the next few years celebrated Formula One like a national festival. So much so that the festivities somewhat overshadowed the race and were, of course, far more enjoyable.

Over the years, I attended a few Formula One races, including one at Silverstone, the original home of motor racing, but nothing quite matched my 1999 experience in Kuala Lumpur. Sadly though, when the novelty of a Grand Prix race wore off, it became more of a routine. The crowds have dwindled over the years and, to a large extent, the appeal is not quite the same.

For all that, the inaugural Malaysian Grand Prix remains a landmark of sorts in my career. If anything, it opened my eyes to a world I never previously knew existed. The event exposed me to the sheer scale of operations, the mind-boggling logistics of transporting hundreds of tons of material around the world, the efficient organisation and detailed planning, right up to the last second.

You got to be there to appreciate Formula One, that is not all about indulging in a pastime while burning millions of dollars on wine, women and song. It can be addictive, as it has been in my case. The howl of the Formula One engine, the wheel-to-wheel racing at over 300 kmph and the omnipresence of danger make for a highly intoxicating mix.

In fact, the 1999 Formula One Malaysian Grand Prix would certainly go down in my book as an event that, in hindsight, put Asia on the world motorsport map with other countries in the region, like Korea, China and India, besides the neighbouring Middle-East, getting on board for a ride that has no equal.

So, as I drove back to the airport on Monday after the race, I could still see all the evidence of a mega, weeklong party that Kuala Lumpur threw while welcoming Formula One in a befitting manner.

Call it a 'miracle' or fate or destiny, I was happy that I was part of the show, at least as an awe-struck spectator, like a million others. Even more so that I was privileged enough to chronicle my visit and the race itself as I began a new chapter in my life.

On my return home, my editor was quite pleased with the coverage and I realised, then, that Formula One had one more convert.

Postscript

A lot of water has flowed down the Klang and Gombak rivers since those heady days of 1999. Kuala Lumpur and Sepang host the Formula One troops as a matter of routine, much like an annual jamboree. While the Sepang International Circuit remains much the same in character, the attendances have certainly fallen, as also the revenues. I have made several trips to the circuit and nothing quite comes close to the excitement of 1999. Like most F1 circuits elsewhere, the returns barely justify spends on hosting the race. But for the continued government support, it is debatable whether the Malaysian Grand Prix would have survived.

Anand Philar has been a sports journalist for over three decades, having worked with *Deccan Herald* and *The New Indian Express* as the Sports Editor, besides Sify Technologies as the Business Manager. He currently heads his Media consultancy firm AP Media Communications and is based in Bengaluru.

The Last of the Romantics

Suresh Menon

> Dravid's retirement has left behind two gaping holes—one in the middle order and another at slip. In this, the natural comparison is probably with Hammond, an elegant batsman with the most famous cover drive in the game and an exceptional catcher at slip, who might have been the greatest batsman of his time but for the arrival of the less elegant but more effective Bradman.

Even in a country obsessed with figures (runs, wickets, IPL millions), it is not widely known that Rahul Dravid scored more runs for India in Test cricket than Sachin Tendulkar since the former made his debut. Or that he played more Tests than the Mumbai man in the same period. Dravid, maker of the second highest number of runs in Test cricket, player of more deliveries than anybody else, is thus judged by effectiveness, style, influence and other such abstract qualities while the digital focus is on Tendulkar.

The nation did not lose sleep over whether Dravid would go past Sunil Gavaskar's thirty-four centuries, and he did it in the evening of a great career with as little fuss as he had begun it with a near-century at Lord's.

In that first Test, Dravid invited both congratulations and commiserations. The one often came with the other in his career. He made ninety-five then and it was impossible to congratulate him without commiserating with him.

To be defined by what he has missed has sometimes been Dravid's fate. When he made 180 in a Test match, he was upstaged by a man who made 281; that innings by VVS Laxman is rated as the best by an Indian batsman. When Dravid made his then highest one-day score of 145, Sourav Ganguly made 183 in the same innings; when he topped that by making 153 against New Zealand, Tendulkar made an unbeaten 186. Is Rahul Dravid the best supporting act in the history of the game or a great player born in the wrong decade? He is the best supporting act in the history of the game—a world record of eighty-five century partnerships in Tests, and a great player—over ten-thousand runs in both forms of the game. It is tempting to conclude that he was born in the wrong decade, forcing him to play in the shadow of Tendulkar, but that hardly mattered to the man who was in competition with no one but himself, and who was secure enough to say at one time, 'Most people want me to get out quickly so they can watch Sachin bat.' Today even the die-hard Tendulkar acolyte would confess that he was willing to wait, for he knew that Dravid getting out early usually spelt disaster. While a Sehwag or a Tendulkar halts life in the nation, with fans dropping whatever they are doing to watch the action, Dravid would let life go on. It is as if his countrymen were saying, adapting Robert Browning, 'Rahul's at the crease, all's right with the world.'

Dravid is the least obtrusive of players, he demands little mind space. He wears his passion on one sleeve, his intelligence on the other. It is a rare combination that evokes awe rather than love, admiration more than conviviality. He is the intelligent man's guide to what a sportsman ought to be—modest, dependable, well-educated, with the gift of grace under pressure and a perspective that is adult. He is the comfort for those who know they cannot be Tendulkar.

While carving out a distinct cricketing personality despite performing alongside Tendulkar, Dravid ensured that the Indian team retained some of the old-fashioned values unique to cricket. For some years after that Kolkata partnership with Laxman, Dravid carried the Indian batting on his shoulders, saving Test matches in Port of Spain, Georgetown and Nottingham and playing the key role in victories in Headingley, Adelaide, Kandy and Rawalpindi. He had four centuries in successive innings and four double centuries in a span of fifteen Tests. He made an incredible 23 per cent of the runs made by India in the twenty-one victories under Ganguly, at an average of 102.84. His overall average crossed Tendulkar's and his wicket became the most sought after.

It is necessary to descend into statistics only to underline the fact that with Dravid it is never beauty without cruelty—he was a stylish batsman who made it count, a do-gooder who was focused on the result, a century-maker whose innings were not out of touch with team performance but an integral part of it. No ploughing the lonely furrow here, every part was a piece of the main. And yet Tendulkar has to be the starting point for any assessment of Dravid, just as Don Bradman was for a study of Walter Hammond, or Gary Sobers for the understanding of Rohan Kanhai. Such men are, to twist a modern usage, the significant others in the careers of batsmen who will appear with an asterisk against their names because a colleague or rival did everything they did, often at a higher level and usually with greater energy.

Had Tendulkar not existed (and it would have been impossible to invent him), we would be singing hosannas to Dravid with the same spontaneity and lack of self-consciousness with which we call Tendulkar god. The media would be holding debates over who the greatest Indian batsman was—Dravid or Gavaskar. After rolling out the clichés (comparisons are odious, and so on) someone digging deeper would unearth the fact that Gavaskar averaged 44 in twenty-three of India's wins while Dravid averaged 65 in fifty-five of India's victories (his average in defeats, 30, gives us a hint of his value). Or that Dravid averaged better abroad than at home or that only four of his thirty-six centuries were made in lost games. There is no finality to any debate in sports, no conclusion that is acceptable to all, which is why revisionism is the favourite pastime of the sports fan. If the statistics do not support a theory, then an appeal is made to a higher element—aesthetics, ethics, effectiveness, charm, team spirit. It is cricket's conceit that a well-made thirty-five full of poetry-provoking strokes is better than a grinding century, that a leg break that spins across the face of the stumps is somehow superior to the one that spins just enough to take the edge of the bat en route to the wicketkeeper.

Of all sports, cricket is the least interested in context, least affected by milieu. Its nature—a series of discrete events making up the whole in fifty overs or five days—makes it possible to isolate individual events and appreciate them without a thought to their relevance to the big picture. In the days when India lost more than they won, such cherry-picking was necessary. When individual performances were divorced from team results, there was consolation in defeat. Australia might have thrashed India, but there was Vijay Hazare's two centuries in the match to celebrate; India might have sunk to a new low against the West Indies, but there was solace in Gavaskar's batting. The great player, however, has both the figures and the aesthetics to show for it. And if there is an essential difference between

Tendulkar and Dravid, technically two of the soundest batsmen of this or any other age, then it is in their choice in the aesthetic debate. Tendulkar, less elaborate in defence, more creative in attack, would place efficiency above style. Dravid, taller, leaner, more stylish, would lay greater store by doing the right thing the right way, the process as important as the product. Tendulkar's batting is a joy of straight lines and geometric precision; Dravid's bat made no angles to the wind and described beautiful arcs. In this, he was the spiritual successor to Gundappa Viswanath, whose secret of the ferocious square cut was passed on to him in that mysterious way cricketing genes jump from one generation to another. Or perhaps it is part of a shared memory as a Karnataka batsman. Long before he was chosen to play for India, Dravid told a colleague, 'I don't want to be just another India player. I want to be bracketed with Gavaskar and Viswanath.' The schoolboy Dravid had photographs taken with his two heroes.

In time he would dine at the high table with them. He played more strokes more consistently than Gavaskar and the more risky ones with greater safety than Viswanath. Alone among his generation he pulled the fast bowler, either standing tall and dismissing the ball with a roll of the wrists or pirouetting to get both the timing and the placement right, and occasionally ending up facing the wicketkeeper. It was only after playing ninety-four Tests in a row since debut that he was forced to miss a game due to illness—a tribute as much to his fitness as to his commitment. What he lacked was an endorsement from someone like Bradman that put the seal on the stature of Tendulkar. Hammond died decades before Dravid was born, and Greg Chappell is of too recent a vintage to put his seal on anyone, especially after his forgettable stint as the Indian coach. There was something of the younger Chappell's elegance in Dravid's driving and his sleek movements against spin. Some years ago, Dravid said that on the off-side, only god had a better drive than Ganguly; well, Ganguly might have returned that compliment, except that god's competition would have been Dravid on the on-side. Mahela Jayawardene alone among modern batsmen plays the leg glance with the assurance of a Dravid, who, in the course of a long innings, suggested that the on-side belonged to him. It was some years before he played with the same confidence on the off-side, but when he retired, he had one of the best cover drives in the game. It has always been thus with Dravid—an initial suggestion of an Achilles' heel followed by hard work and then emergence as the best in the field. This is as true of the cover drive as of one-day cricket, and more recently the Twenty20 version. Dravid's father and uncle were both cricketers and to them, as to Rahul, cricket is more than a game, it is a philosophy. This is an attitude Dravid has occasionally had to pay a price for.

Early in his career, he made it clear he was prepared to bat at any slot for India, keep wickets if necessary and probably prepare the pitch, paint the stadium and man the car park, too. His involvement in the game was total. This kind of focus is old-fashioned, obsessive and difficult for an outsider to understand in anyone over twelve years of age. Both Tendulkar and Dravid brought that passion into their game, their idea of the perfect day not very different from their normal day playing cricket, batting on and on. But while Tendulkar dominates through attack, Dravid was content to let his domination remain a secret between the bowler and himself. Only the discerning could tell that he had the bowler on the run, there were no great flashes or overt gestures of aggression. Like a great actor, Dravid preferred to underplay his role, made his impact by understatement, and occasionally let the bowler run out of steam by the sureness of his defence. His nickname—the Wall—is inappropriate, though, and not one he likes. A wall is a passive thing, letting things happen to it. It merely blocks an enemy advance without repelling it. Dravid's was not a passive resistance; rather, it was a calculated strategy employed in the knowledge that his strength, both physical and mental, was superior to the bowler's. And he was not merely looking to block an advance. He took the fight to the enemy camp.

Test cricket came naturally to Dravid, as it did to Gavaskar before him, Vijay Hazare and Vijay Merchant before that. It is tempting to imagine that the quintessential 'Dravidness' was to be found in the longer form of the game. Yet, it was in overcoming his initial unsuitability for one-day cricket and finding a slot for himself as a leading player in that format that he exhibited the qualities of head and heart that made him special. It was a mental leap that Gavaskar could not make; Hazare and Merchant didn't need to. Dravid had to work harder at gaining acceptance in the shorter format. Dravid did not turn his nose up at it like Gavaskar did, he merely accepted it as part of the game he loved and was professional enough to adapt to it. In the early days, the selectors, media, administrators, even players were united on one thing: Dravid was no one-day batsman. He had the shots but could be kept quiet over long periods by setting an orthodox field. He seldom played over the top. And on good tracks he didn't play on the rise, like Tendulkar or Ganguly. At least that was the theory. In his first year of international cricket, Dravid had a highest score of ninety in one-dayers and a respectable average of around 28 from 20 matches. Next year he had a century against Pakistan and an average of 40. But now came the intrigue, never far from the surface in Indian cricket. He was told that since the team had stroke players of the calibre of Tendulkar, Mohammad Azharuddin, Ganguly, Ajay Jadeja and others, his role was to keep one end going and bat through fifty overs. He followed his instructions so well, concentrating on keeping his wicket, that he was dropped for his falling strike rate. He was labelled and dismissed—a classic Indian gambit. However, once Dravid fought his way back for the World Cup in 1999, he emerged as a fine all-round one-day batsman, playing the angles well and unafraid to loft the ball. He was the leading scorer with 461 runs, two centuries, an average of 66 and a strike rate of 86. Soon he became a wonderful floater in the batting line-up, with specific roles while opening, playing at three or lower down as insurance policy to see the side home in a chase. Despite not liking the job, he kept wickets too, for it enabled India to play the extra batsman or bowler as the occasion demanded.

One-day cricket also brought out the difference between Viswanath and Dravid. The former became increasingly orthodox in the latter part of his career, a change necessitated by advancing age and slower reflexes. Viswanath changed his guard from leg to middle stump and began playing straighter. Dravid went in the opposite direction. He discovered aspects of himself that may have remained hidden but for the dictates of the one-day game. He gradually freed himself from the shackles of excessive orthodoxy and began playing a more creative game, secure in the knowledge that you must first master the rules before you can attempt to break them. Such has been the effect of the one-day game on an intelligent mind. After all, there are only nine positions that can be blocked on a cricket field (if you take away the bowler and the wicketkeeper). This means there are bound to be gaps that cannot be manned. The arc between mid-on and midwicket became a Dravid favourite, as did the open space to the left of cover point. If the captain rearranged the field to plug these holes, Dravid had enough variation to place the ball in other untenanted areas. He surprised fast bowlers like Allan Donald by driving them back over their head for six and sent leg spinners into a tailspin by flicking the ball from outside the off stump wide of midwicket for four. These were shots born of confidence and the understanding of the angles on a cricket field. When he took over as captain, Dravid emphasised the importance of enjoying the game.

Like the American constitution, he laid great store in the pursuit of happiness. This is unusual in a modern captain who understands victory and defeat but not too many things beyond. Dravid's insistence on relaxing and enjoying the game was good strategy, too. For, as he has said, you cannot perform unless you are relaxed. When he gave up captaincy after the England tour, following a series of unhappy encounters with the then chairman of selectors, he was following in the footsteps of Tendulkar, who gave it up because much as he loved the job, he hated the politics that went with it.

There might be debates over who the greatest Indian batsman is, or which of the spinners deserves to be No 1. But one such assertion is beyond argument—that Dravid is the greatest slip fielder we have had. And in keeping with both the character of the game and the character of the man himself, it is not something that has used up column inches in newspapers or whatever it is that is used up in cyberspace. As the first non-wicketkeeper with 200 catches, Dravid's place in the Pantheon is assured. He was not a flashy catcher at slip—his anticipation got him into position quickly and there was no need for desperate lunges or dramatic dives—but few edges went past. He was superbly balanced, and a study in the art of positioning, especially against the spinners. That one hundred of his catches came off the Anil Kumble-Harbhajan Singh combination underlines the crucial role he played in the careers of India's two most successful spinners.

There was something special about Dravid at slip. In the one-day game, he was happy to stand wider than normal, but in Tests he was the orthodox fielder, taking his bearings from the batsman and the extension of the return crease.

Dravid's retirement left behind two gaping holes—one in the middle order and another at slip. In this, the natural comparison is probably with Hammond, an elegant batsman with the most famous cover drive in the game and an exceptional catcher at slip who might have been the greatest batsman of his time, but for the arrival of the less elegant but more effective Bradman. Dravid is the old-fashioned modern steeped in the history and legends of the game, as opposed to, say, Sehwag, who famously said after nearly breaking Vinoo Mankad's world record partnership for the first wicket that he hadn't heard of Mankad. Cricket is one of the few sports where the term 'old-fashioned' is a compliment. Rafael Nadal, for instance, would be insulted if you called him an old-fashioned tennis player. It is a quirk of the language, and perhaps of the game itself, that 'old-fashioned' does not mean hidebound, inflexible or anything negative. It describes a player who uses traditional methods to meet modern challenges, someone who understands the grammar of the game and uses it to compose its essays. Dravid, who has the best record among the modern old-fashioned ones, once said he was constantly amazed that he was being paid to do what he loved doing best. Every profession has the uber-professional, one who is looked up to by his peers, and commands their respect for the ability to do things that even the best among them struggle to. And it is not just about skill, although that is important too. It is about temperament, about discipline and the ability to get out of trouble when the going gets rough. For nearly a decade and a half, Dravid played that role in Indian cricket. Tendulkar's genius is of an order that the average player cannot comprehend. Dravid's greatness is not just comprehensible, it is reassuring. The Tendulkars of the cricketing world appear but rarely, and when they leave, it is generally accepted that the gap can never be filled. It is the Gavaskars and Dravids who spawn successors. Dravid might have to wait before his true worth is realised, and his incredible contribution to Indian cricket fully acknowledged. He is a man of infinite patience, and is unlikely to be in any hurry.

Postscript

Rahul Dravid was probably ready for Test cricket a couple of seasons before he actually played; at thirty-nine, as the then oldest player in the world, he was easily among the fittest Indians. It is safe to assume that he will never bid goodbye to the game despite being one of the few players with interests beyond it. The media suggests itself, and Dravid could develop into a serious writer on the game in the class of England's Michael Atherton. Dravid is the well-read, big-picture man who will be a dignified chief of the ICC. He has much more to contribute to the game, of that there is no doubt.

Suresh Menon, editor, *Wisden India Almanack*, has been writing on the game for over a quarter century. He was one of the country's youngest newspaper editors. His books include, *Sachin: Genius Unplugged* (editor), *Champions: How the World Cup was Won* and *Bishan: Portrait of a Cricketer*.

Index